Lost Souls: FOUND!™

Inspiring Stories About Golden Retrievers

Kyla Duffy and Lowrey Mumford

Published by Happy Tails Books™, LLC

Happy Tails Books™ publishes breed-specific and region-specific compilations of stories about rescued dogs. These thought-provoking books are meant to entertain pet lovers, and raise awareness about pet adoption and typical breed characteristics. They provide a venue for proud owners to showcase their adopted pets and generate funding for rescue groups through the donation of a portion of each sale.

Lost Souls: FOUND!™

Inspiring Stories About Golden Retrievers by Kyla Duffy and Lowrey Mumford

Published by Happy Tails Books™, LLC   www.happytailsbooks.com

The publisher gratefully acknowledges the numerous Golden Retriever rescue groups and their members who generously granted permission to use their stories and photos.

Front cover photo:
Buddy, by Tim Hancock, timhancockphoto@juno.com
Back cover photos:
Buddy, Zamboni and Cody, by Tim Hancock
Cooper by Michelle Enebo www.enebophotoblog.com
Interior photos unassociated with a story:
Interior Title Page and P 7: Yogi, by Tim Hancock
P 12: Mariah by Karen Taylor, www.pawsinthegarden.com
Just Fur Fun Pages: Chester by Lani Doely
www.lanidoelyphotography.com

Publishers Cataloging In Publication

Lost Souls: FOUND!™ Inspiring Stories About Golden Retrievers/ [Compiled and edited by] Kyla Duffy and Lowrey Mumford.

p. ; cm.

ISBN: 978-0-9824895-1-2

1. Golden Retriever. 2. Dog rescue. 3. Dogs – Anecdotes. 4. Animal welfare – United States. 5. Human-animal relationships – Anecdotes. I. Duffy, Kyla. II. Mumford, Lowrey. III. Title.

SF426.5   2010

636.7527-dc21   2009906764

Thank you to all of the contributors and rescue groups whose thought-provoking stories make this book come to life!

Arizona Golden Retriever Connection
http://www.azgrc.org/

Everglades Golden Retriever Rescue, Inc.
http://www.egrr.org/

Evergreen Golden Retriever Rescue
http://www.egrr.net/

Golden Rescue South Florida
http://www.goldenrescuesouthflorida.com/

Golden Retriever Freedom Rescue
http://www.goldenretrieverfreedom.com/

Golden Retriever Rescue of Atlanta
http://www.grra.com/

Golden Retriever Rescue and Adoption of Needy Dogs
http://www.grrand.org/

Golden Retriever Rescue of Wisconsin
http://www.grrow.org/

Golden Treasures Golden Retriever Rescue
http://www.goldentreasuresrescue.org/

Great Lakes Golden Retriever Rescue
http://www.petfinder.com/shelters/MI377.html

Love A Golden Rescue
http://www.loveagolden.com/

Tennessee Valley Golden Retriever Rescue
http://www.tvgrr.com/

Table of Contents

Introduction: Answering the Call.. ix

More Interesting than Shoes...14

Furry Gold Medicine..17

The Barreling Humper..21

A Series of Firsts..25

That Dog IS Family...29

Good Things Come to Those Who Wait......................................33

Santa's Helpers...36

Just Fur Fun!..40

How Oprah Saved Gracie...41

The Royal Treatment...45

Voodoo Magic...47

Challenge is a Chariot...52

A Yellow Ribbon for My Son...54

A Jessie of All Trades...56

Every Breath You Take...60

Hardships Can Draw Us Closer..63

Just Fur Fun!..66

Little Brother Grows Up..67

"Tripp" of a Lifetime...70

Imperfect Is Perfect...73

In Sickness and in Health..75

Just for a Week 79

No White Flag Needed 83

Just Fur Fun!...87

Who's Your Daddy?..88

A Beautiful Challenge 91

"Lola, Who?" 94

Aloha, In Every Sense of the Word.....................................97

Now She Laughs Out Loud 101

The Relationship Between Dog and Human......................104

Just Fur Fun!...107

Must a "Real" Golden Retrieve?..108

Nose to the Ground 111

The "If's" Would Have Been Easy.......................................114

Little Orphan Antics...119

Nat-the-Cat 122

Little Time, Big Love 125

Dry Toast..128

Wet Toast..129

Because Giving Them Up Is a Gift 131

A Golden's Favorite Treat 137

Golden Learning Opportunities 138

To Save One..140

Give me your dog tired, your dog-eared,
Your huddled masses yearning to go home again,
The wretched refuse of the dog-eat-dog world.
Send these, the homeless, tempest-tossed to me,
I lift my lamp beside the golden door!
Stephen Guy

Introduction: Answering the Call

I t was very early on the morning of my second wedding anniversary, so I didn't answer the phone when it rang. I wanted to sleep in with my hubby. When I finally checked voicemail, it was the president of the rescue group I foster for. The message simply said, "They found Bill. Call me."

I should have answered the call.

Bill was my two-year-old train wreck of a foster, who I had only for an hour before he and another little girl I was fostering escaped from my yard. Well-socialized to people, the girl was found and returned immediately, but we were afraid Bill was gone for good. Terrified of people and completely unsocialized from spending his life in a cage at a puppy mill, we knew he would try to get as far away from humans as possible. Three weeks passed, and I feared the coyotes had caught him, so the call that morning was shocking, to say the least. It was also ambiguous. Was he found alive? Dead? Where was he?

Joggers saw Bill in the woods about a quarter of a mile from my home, splayed out on a trail, trying to eat a carcass. They alerted animal control, who took him to our local Humane Society. His microchip was scanned, and he was subsequently reunited with our group.

Bill's future was uncertain. His three-week ordeal left him with a gash on his leg so deep that his muscle was exposed, and he was down to 13 lbs. from 21, leaving his every bone protruding. He just sat, unresponsive, no light in his eyes. His mood seemed similar to when I first got him, but physically he was much worse. Needless to say, I was overwhelmed with remorse, but also driven to help him however I could, no matter what it would take.

For a month I took him to the vet every other day to get his bandages changed. For three months, my husband and I hoped that he would start to move. Bill was so scared; he just sat in his bed and cowered. We carried him outside to potty, and then he would dart back to his bed. For a while we thought he would do best as a companion for a shut-in who did not have much activity in his or her home. However, after a time, Bill finally started to come around, and we decided that the best place for him was right here in our home.

With training (by my husband and me, and by the dogs at the dog park), Bill started to gain confidence and understanding. He realized that we are here to love him, and that he is supposed to play and enjoy life. We've discovered that he loves hiking and romping through fields with other dogs, so we get him his "own" dog to foster as often as possible. Sometimes he's the big brother, and other times the fosters mentor him. Either way, it's always a great experience for us all.

Working with rescue groups (especially after Bill's fiasco) has given me much to reflect on. I cringe when I think about my best friend Bill's life at the puppy mill and lost in the woods. For a while, I felt completely helpless when considering the millions of other dogs also living without love, shelter, or proper medical care. Then one day in my heart I "heard the call," and I wasn't going to miss it again. I realized that feeling helpless was not going to save lives.

However, publishing books full of stories about wonderful adopted dogs, and the positive impact they have had on their families, just might. This is how the "Lost Souls: FOUND!" book series was born.

If you read carefully, you'll surely laugh, cry, and learn from these amazing stories submitted by fosters and forever families, just as my co-editor Lowrey and I did when we edited them. I hope they will reinforce the belief that rescued dogs are exceptional dogs and are certainly worth the effort.

When you're finished reading, ask yourself if you've heard the call to support rescue. Volunteering, donating, or just sharing information are all valuable ways to help.

If you hear the call, don't let it go to voicemail. "Pick up the phone" and save a life.

Kyla Duffy, Editor

Inspiring Stories About Golden Retrievers

Woof, woof, woof....bark, bark!

More Interesting than Shoes

"The key," she said softly, "is to be more interesting than whatever he's looking at."

It was 9:00 a.m., and I was crouched on the floor of my local PETCO® with the trainer, and a statue that had moments earlier been a four-year-old Golden Retriever named Eli. We were at an obedience class where we had been working on "loose leash walking," and he'd been doing quite well, actually. At least he had been until he saw the ferrets. Despite my best efforts, for ten minutes after Eli first laid eyes on them, he stood completely still, not blinking, totally impervious to my gentle nudges, my excited calls, my offers of a treat. Nothing would break his gaze. The trainer remarked that in all her years she'd never seen a dog quite like Eli.

Nor, for that matter, had I. My family and I were lucky enough to have three Goldens, even before I got Eli during my first year of law school. While all of them had displayed a "love" of nature, if you will, none came close to Eli.

Instead of playing ball or swimming, Eli prefers sitting at the window of my apartment for hours on end, watching the birds and the squirrels. Rather than playing with the dogs at my girlfriend's house, he chooses to sit at the porch door and scan her backyard. At my parents' house he spends half of his time outside, lying and watching the animals. Long periods of calm are punctuated by sudden bursts of energy, where he runs across the yard at full speed, trying to catch one that strayed too far afield. The other half of his time is spent sitting in front of my parents' birdcage, drooling all over himself and occasionally looking up at me, wondering when I will open the cage and let him do his job.

Looking back, Toby (Eli's name, at the time) was more than hesitant the first time I met him, and I don't think I could have imagined then that he would grow into the dog I today know and love as Eli. As much as Eli's not a "normal" Golden Retriever, having him has brought order to my mildly chaotic life. Gone are the days of sleeping until two in the afternoon and staying at the library to study for 14 hours straight. Gone is the freedom to leave food lying around at dog-on-his-hind-legs-height or to just stay inside all day when it is cold or snowy.

But also gone is the feeling of coming home to an empty apartment. Gone is waking up and having no one to greet me. I suddenly have my very own, foolproof, smile machine, which can cheer me up no matter how down I may feel. There's nothing like laughing at him rolling around on the floor while attacking a stuffed goose or taking him on a good, long walk. There are few things in this world which can brighten your world like a happy dog, and Eli's endless energy and constant enthusiasm lighten whatever load the day may have built up on my shoulders.

No matter Eli's current distraction, he never lets me forget he is around. He slides around on the hardwood floor and pounces on toys when I throw them in the air. Whenever I try to put on my shoes, he always sits on my feet, making sure, it seems, I don't forget he wants to join me wherever I'm going. While he may have appeared to be stuck on the ferrets, he must have actually been listening when the trainer said, "The key is to be more interesting than whatever he's looking at."

 *Jon Markman*

Furry Gold Medicine

Becky was the smelliest Golden Retriever that the rescue group had ever seen. Her skin was black and she hardly had any fur. Regardless, I wanted her. The only problem was that another family had gotten to her first.

We ended up adopting a male instead, and things turned out very well for us. Unfortunately, they did not go so well for Becky, who was placed back into rescue a few months after her adoption. The family's excuse was that Becky was an incorrigible counter surfer who had also tried to chew her way through a door. She attempted to eat from a pot of hot chili and broke all her teeth trying to escape from her crate.

When I called again to adopt her, I was informed that Becky now had no muscle mass, had lost about twenty pounds, and was again missing much of her fur. The rescue vet determined that she was starving due to a bad case of hookworms, which explained the counter surfing behavior. She also had a recurrence of her horrible skin condition, causing her skin to turn black with an elephant-like appearance. She was bald from her chin to her belly, had a yeast infection, and had numerous unspecified allergies. She was now considered a "special needs" adoption.

Still, we wanted to meet Becky. We visited her three times in December and learned that she would have to be given a special diet, nutritional supplements, and twice-weekly medicated baths. The vet said she wasn't certain if Becky was incontinent because he had noticed an odor of urine in her living space. If incontinence were an issue, she would have to be on medication for that as well. Were we up for it? You bet we were.

On New Year's Eve, Becky came home with us as a foster-to-adopt. At first she was aloof, looking for corners where she could lie down and be undisturbed. She did not trust anyone. She would go out for short walks but not for long distances. At night she would find her way into an extra bathroom and relieve herself on the bathroom rug.

She raided the trash and devoured anything she could get: Paper towels used for draining grilled chicken? She gobbled them down. Corncobs? No problem! Banana peels? Yum!

We moved and secured the trash to another room, but with the trash unavailable, Becky returned to counter surfing. Apples waiting to be placed in lunch boxes were no challenge for Becky. She could make a large apple disappear in three bites. Groceries, we learned quickly, needed to be put away with haste, and prepared foods had to be consumed immediately.

Becky was a good teacher, and before long we learned to be good parents. We discovered something special underneath that smelly exterior, and we adopted Becky a month after she moved in with us. It took a year, but with nutritious food, daily supplements, routine baths, massages, and grooming, Becky became a more beautiful dog - a poster child for Golden Retriever rescue, at least on the surface.

Yet Becky still seemed sad. Each Saturday morning, we would leave with our other Golden to visit the elderly at an assisted living facility and a nursing home. Becky started showing interest in accompanying us and would follow us to the door with a wagging tail. We told her she had to stay and went off without her. Becky's tail would stop wagging, but she would still be waiting at the door when we returned home two hours later.

Each week it became more difficult to get out the door without Becky. By this time Becky was about nine years old, but we decided to attempt to get her certified to do pet-assisted therapy.

Becky was still difficult to walk on a leash, and the trash-raiding behavior never really ceased, so we tried to resolve those issues in obedience classes. After six weeks of training, Becky passed Basic Obedience. I was still not sure if she would pass the test to become a therapy dog, but we kept practicing anyway. Then, on Valentine's Day, to my astonishment and delight, Becky passed her test on the first attempt! She got her very own vest and began her new mission.

Each week, we now travel as a foursome to three facilities. The residents eagerly await our arrival. Becky is popular because she likes to put her head on the residents' laps and lovingly gaze into their eyes. If someone stops petting before Becky is ready, she will put her paw on his or her hand, as if to say, "Please don't stop."

On a recent Saturday, we were visiting with Ruth, a patient at a nursing home. As Becky was entertaining Ruth with her trademark charm, a medical professional approached. "Is that Ruth?" he asked. "I can't believe it! I saw her just the other day for an evaluation and she seemed almost despondent. Now she's happy like I have never seen her before. I guess pets are better therapy than medical professionals."

In Becky's case I quite agree. It's obvious that her visits with the elderly residents are some kind of cure, at least for "the blues!" It's furry Golden medicine – rescue one or two, and call me in the morning!

 *Marie Foley*

The Barreling Humper

*C*lassified Ad: "11-month-old Golden Retriever, free to good home. Crate included."

My husband, Paul, and I had three rescued cats, but I wanted a dog. I grew up with dogs, but Paul had not, so he took some convincing. There were no more excuses. We no longer lived in an apartment, we had a cabin with a small fenced yard, my boys from a previous marriage were grown, and since Paul was traveling frequently for work I was lonely.

My last dog had died shortly before Paul and I met. Over the years I'd scanned the classifieds for a dog and picked up the phone to call, but never did. Finally, now I could follow through.

"I'm calling about your ad for the Golden," I said.

The guy on the other end replied, "He's terrible, but if you want to meet him...."

Apparently the man's ex-wife had given him a puppy as a surprise Christmas present, but they had never bonded. He said the dog had bad hips, was fat, untrained, and terrible; I probably wouldn't want him. I insisted on meeting him anyway.

I told Paul I was going to look at a dog, but that was it... nothing about the bad hips. In fact, I didn't tell him anything that the guy had told me. Instead, I just described general positive attributes that would convince my husband we would adopt this golden boy.

After work I went alone to meet my new dog. I followed the perfect brick path to the front door, where the man asked me to leave my shoes - it was winter and apparently he didn't want anything tracked in. He led me through the immaculate living room, carpeted in white, past the little Scotties that were allowed in the house, and down the stairs into the damp basement. As he opened the door, he said, "He'll probably hump you; he's a terrible dog."

Sure enough, as I stepped through the door and onto the cold concrete floor, I was practically bowled over by a huge Golden, barreling towards me at full-speed! As he humped my leg and chewed on my forearm, I looked around the sterile room, bare except for a dog crate, food bowl, and water bowl. Through the sliding glass doors, I could see that the Scotties had a wonderful yard to play in, so why was this Golden stuck in the basement like this?

There was no way I was leaving him there. I said, "I want him," I leashed him, and up the stairs we flew! I almost fell as he pulled me along the icy path and then screeched to a halt at the car. I opened the door and said, "Hop up," but he stood his ground and wouldn't get in.

The guy said, "I never took him anywhere," and just went back in the house, leaving me to shove this obese Golden into my backseat by myself. I left the crate on the sidewalk, drove away, and in less than a block had a happy dog in the front with me, head out the window, loving life!

Since Paul was working in town that week, I stopped at his jobsite to introduce him to his new dog. With me on the end of the leash, the dog dragged me, slipping and sliding, through the mud. He flung me through the door of the unfinished home addition my husband was working on, and we came to an ungraceful stop at Paul's feet. Shocked, Paul appraised his new overweight, unruly, and matted Golden. The poor dog was so fat that his belly rolled from side to side when he ran!

I said, "Hi, Honey! Here's our new dog."

Should I have described him a little more accurately when I asked Paul if we could take him? Possibly, but oops, too late, he was *ours*!

We named the dog Pierce, after Pierce Brosnan, as Paul is a huge James Bond fan. Mr. Brosnan was an appropriate namesake since he, too, had a rough start in life, but stuck it out to be a successful, happy man (and pretty nice looking too – just like our Pierce turned out to be!).

During his first few months with us, Pierce tore up t-shirts, chewed up a couch, stole apple pies, distressed cats, and peed on beds. No shower was complete without Pierce either in it with us or tearing down the curtain to make sure we were there!

Four years later, Pierce hikes and swims and loves all the things any Golden should. Instead of shredding T-shirts, he chews tennis balls and plays endless fetch, which has helped him shrink from a hefty 135 lbs. to a healthy 86 lbs.

I love my formerly obese, unruly, arthritic, hip-dysplasia-affected, barreling humper and wouldn't have him any other way!

 *Shereen Raucci*

A Series of Firsts

I am a retired air force colonel, and I experienced many "firsts" in my 28-year career, including surviving the attack on the Pentagon on 9/11. However, no "first" in my life prepared me for my first year with Howie.

Howie was rescued from a puppy mill in Missouri and brought to Colorado along with 21 other dogs. If you're not familiar with puppy mills, they are large-scale breeding farms where dogs are kept in small, wire cages without attention or proper medical care. The breeding dogs, and their puppies (who are usually sold to unsuspecting dog-lovers through pet stores, newspaper ads, or online), end up with severe psychological and/or physical trauma. And so it was with our Howie...

Golden Retriever Freedom Rescue (GRFR) graciously took Howie in, even though he was one of the worst cases of puppy mill abuse they had seen. He was underweight, and his lower teeth were missing, either from chewing on his cage for two years or they may have been filed off by the miller (yes, people who own puppy mills actually do that). His foster family worked with him daily for many long months, just to be able to do the most basic regular dog stuff like put on his collar.

Regardless of his past, something about Howie's soulful, golden-yellow eyes told me he was the one. So my husband, Doug, and I took a chance and adopted him. This was our first time adopting a puppy mill dog and was just the beginning of a series of firsts!

The first night with Howie was a shock. He leapt our four-and-a-half foot fence with ease and, just as we were about to start combing the neighborhood, returned stealthily through the fence gate. It turns out that the fight-or-flight reaction is a natural instinct for dogs that have been caged and neglected for their entire lives. We were grateful and relieved that Howie somehow decided that we could be trusted.

We spent those first few days discovering how deeply troubled Howie was and felt helpless to deal with his special needs. He was scared of everything and missed the security of his foster family's home. He was testing us. GRFR suggested we clip his leash to our belts and have him follow us around the house - an amazing little suggestion that put Howie on track to becoming a well-adjusted dog.

Going on walks seemed almost painful and frightening for Howie. He had never been outside of a cage to experience pine trees, squirrels, deer, and all the wonderful smells nature has to offer. The first time he stopped to sniff, six months after he'd been with us, was a momentous occasion.

Howie was also frightened of doors. He learned to use our dog door to get out fairly quickly, but he took a while to master the concept of getting back in. He knew very well how to use it but was stubborn and simply stayed outside no matter what we did. The first time Howie came in the door by himself we were elated!

The simple act of feeding treats to Howie was a major undertaking. He was too fearful to take anything from our hands, so we had to put them on the floor and leave (don't dare look at him). The first time he took a treat from my hand was better than winning the lottery!

Guests were another issue. We kept Howie's leash on him by the front door so people could say hello, which he endured with his head down and his tail tucked between his legs. As soon as we took his leash off, he dashed for the dog door and stayed outside until our friends left. Nevertheless, we continued this ritual in hopes of showing Howie that not all people are bad. Eventually, it worked, and he is now our official greeter. The first time he not only stayed around, but actually went up to our guests to sniff and nuzzle his big Goldie head in their hands, all of our hearts melted.

A year after adopting Howie, we went to GRFR's annual reunion and picnic. This was to be Howie's first time off leash in such a big area, and our first reunion picnic. My jaw dropped when I saw the hundreds of Goldens of all shapes, sizes and colors, frolicking and swimming and running. We didn't know how Howie would react, but we cautiously let him off leash... The result was that he turned into Muffasa – the Lion King! His white Golden fur, huge lion-like paws, massive head, and mesmerizing eyes captivated everyone. He looked so majestic - King of the Goldens - and Cindy, his original foster-mom, could not believe it was the same dog she took in. It made us all cry - we were so happy!

We've experienced many rewarding "firsts" with our Howie these past four years: the first time he jumped in the back of our Jeep by himself; the first time he came upstairs at night by himself to go to bed; the first time he came to greet us when we got home from work; the first time he nuzzled his big Golden head in our side while we were walking.

Now we call Howie our Ambassador – no matter where we go, from the beaches of South Carolina to the dog parks of Colorado, everyone asks about Howie. He's inspired others to adopt puppy mill dogs and have their own education of "firsts" like we did... has he inspired you?

 *Ann and Doug Shippy*

That Dog IS Family

As a dog transport volunteer for Golden Retriever Rescue and Adoption of Needy Dogs (GRRAND), I'd take rescued dogs from Lexington, KY to Louisville, KY, where they would reside in foster homes until they could be adopted by a loving family. One of my transport rules was I always put the dogs in the back seat of my Toyota Avalon instead of the front seat, so as not to get attached. I had lost my own Golden, Sassy was her name, two years before. I spent a month with her at Auburn University while she underwent radiation treatments for her seizures, and I still lost her thirty days after returning home. Even after two years I wasn't ready for another dog of my own.

The Retriever I transported from Lexington on this particular day had been scheduled for immediate euthanization at a pound in West Virginia. A Collie rescuer who was at the facility spotted her, called GRRAND, and facilitated the dog's release. From there she began her 200-mile journey to Louisville. The first stop was Portsmouth, Ohio, followed by multiple stops in Kentucky, one of which was me. I was to take her for a forty-minute drive from Lexington to Frankfort, and in Frankfort she would meet her final transport to Louisville.

When it was time, I met the drop-off person at a convenience store parking lot to transfer this absolutely beautiful, red Golden Retriever to my car. I was told they had no history on her, other than she had almost been euthanized. They rescued her, and they named her Brook. Underweight, totally confused, and exhausted, she cowered when I spoke to her and never took her eyes off me, not even for even a second.

Brook looked so pitiful that I broke my rule and put her in the front seat. I rubbed and scratched her soft fur behind her ears and talked to her the whole way, saying over and over, "It's going to be alright."

About five miles into our trip, Brook began to inch her front legs and upper body toward the console between the seats. Soon she was across the console, and within five minutes she had her front legs and head resting on my right leg as I drove. She never licked me, never uttered a sound; she just rolled her sad eyes and stared at me with a longing, desperate stare that made my heart speed up and my emotions bottom out. Who would abuse and abandon such a beautiful, loving dog?

The GRRAND volunteer who met me in Frankfurt to assist with Brook's final transfer took one look at Brook and me, and said, "You're going to take that dog, aren't you?"

I vowed I wouldn't, but I couldn't stop staring at Brook while the lady and I talked. When the volunteer tried to take Brook for a potty break, she refused to move, so I took the leash and easily led her up the hillside. When I then loaded Brook into the volunteer's van, she looked so betrayed and hurt. I felt terrible, and I'll never forget her sad eyes.

That day Brook adopted me, I didn't adopt her. Four days later, the necessary paperwork, home visit, and shots from the GRRAND veterinarian were in order, and I returned to Louisville to be reunited with my beautiful Brook.

Though Brook came to me with many issues, she has since come a long way. My veterinarian estimated that she was barely one year old when I got her; and my trainer, who confirmed my suspicion that Brook was abused, surmised that she had either been chained up or caged and most likely beaten. This poor girl had been through a lot in a short period of time. Nevertheless, she's gone from growling warnings at strangers, to barking for pats from anyone. She still has socialization issues with other dogs, (probably from having to defend her turf in the past), but I take her to some pastureland near my house daily, where she loves to explore and dig up moles. Her rate of (how do I put this nicely) annihilation is now at fifty-six moles!

The love and companionship Brook and I share cannot be described in a short story. We are inseparable. She is my best friend, following me from room to room, even if I only go for a drink of water. She sleeps by my bed, and she is beside me as I am writing this piece. I'm grateful that Brook adopted me that day, and my hope is that others get to experience the joy of "being adopted" by a special needs dog as well. You'll never regret it, and your loving pet will always be loyal to you in so many ways.

Sometimes people say, "That dog is just like family, isn't she?"

With Brook that's not the case. My firm reply is, "No, she *IS* family." In fact, it doesn't get any more "family" than Brook and me.

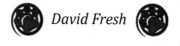

David Fresh

Good Things Come to Those Who Wait

For thirteen years my kids asked for a puppy, and for thirteen years the answer was, "No." I knew the dog would become my responsibility, and everyone else would wash their hands of it, which I didn't think was fair to me, or the dog. Then, one day, after thirteen years of resistance, something must have changed because I finally felt compelled to say, "Yes."

I had periodically visited the Everglades Golden Retriever Rescue (EGRR) website, and was fascinated and touched by the stories of the dogs that came into the Rescue. Perhaps that website is what changed my mind about getting a dog. When I agreed to get a dog, I immediately knew I wanted to adopt one from EGRR.

However, as my husband started reading up on the breed, he insisted we should get a puppy from a good breeder. He shared the horror stories he read about hip dysplasia and all other problems that Golden's are prone to. This is why we got Sunny, a beautiful female puppy, from a reputable breeder.

As much as we loved Sunny, I still couldn't get EGRR out of my mind, and I still wanted to be involved with rescue somehow. When Sunny was nine months old, I filled out a volunteer application.

Initially, I figured I could help with clerical tasks, events, and their website, but it wasn't long before I became a foster. My first dog was Logan, who was in my house for a week before getting adopted by a wonderful family. He had clearly been on his own a while, as he had some scars on his face and head. Yet he was appreciative, gentle, well-mannered, and excellent on the leash. When Logan left my house, I was a wreck. I knew he was going to a good home, but I was acutely aware of his absence.

A couple of days later I was asked to visit a newly surrendered pup named Buddy. He was just turning one, and was at the office of one of our cooperating vets. Initially, I went to take pictures of Buddy for the website, but knowing there was no available foster home for him, I just brought him home with me.

I thought fostering Buddy would help me get over the "loss" I felt from Logan being gone, but Buddy had different plans. He and Sunny got along great, and he immediately showed me what a "mamma's boy" he was. Needless to say, his picture and story never made it to the EGRR website, and he never left our home.

We all love Buddy, and find it very funny that even though we were not going to adopt a dog to begin with, buying one instead, we adopted a dog anyway!

Having dogs and working with the Rescue has helped me discover a personal passion and feeling of purpose that I never experienced before. EGRR and the dogs I have been blessed to help and love have given my soul simple but priceless rewards time and time again.

 *Valentina*

Santa's Helpers

My name is Kona and Arizona Golden Retriever Rescue (AZGRC) brought me to the North Pole to live with Annie B., Santa Claus, and his missus.

Yep, I kid you not, the first time I saw them and got real close to Santa, I saw that his beard was as white as snow - the real thing! When he bent over, I could tell by the twinkle in his eyes and those rosy, chipmunk cheeks, I wasn't dreaming.

His wife had the same snow white hair, and when she saw me, all she could say was, "Oh, Santa, she's just beautiful!"

Before they adopted me, I was shipped from home to home, thinking each home would be my last. I tried so hard to love them all. I was so lonely, I never thought I'd find a real family to make happy. It was also SO hot in the desert, and I was kept outside so much. I really wanted to come inside and be cool, but nobody else seemed to care.

When Santa and his missus came to meet me in my foster home, it was great. "This is it," I thought, "I'm going to the North Pole where it's cool, there are lots of Elves to play with, and life will be good." I was so ready to jump into the sleigh and take off, but instead, they kissed me on the top of my head and then were gone! I was crushed, confused, and heartbroken. I couldn't figure out what I could have done to make them change their minds.

Later that week, two gals came over, picked up my bag of food, grabbed my torn, shredded toy (my only possession), and we left. When I got into the car, things seemed different somehow; the two of them were laughing and petting me. It was as if they were trying to make me feel like "one of the girls," but by now, I knew that I had no control of my life. All I wanted was for them to just get it over with and drop me off "wherever."

We drove so far that there was no more desert, the temperature got cooler, and I couldn't get over the fact that there were big tall trees, mountains, and more open space than I had ever seen. Could this be the North Pole? Not with my luck!

The car stopped; there he was. It was Santa! I came to find out that the little girl next to him, half my size with a tail that just wouldn't stay still, was my new sister Annie B. Inside the house, Annie B. showed me her huge toy box and her "den." She told me I could sleep in the huge, cushy bed for as long as I wanted. When Mrs. Claus saw me, there were more kisses, and I was beginning to feel that I could stay here forever where I was so welcome.

"Not so fast," I kept telling myself... I was just waiting for the girls to grab my stuff and take me away. "But wait," I thought, "....where are those girls?" I looked around and realized that they were gone. It was just the four of us!

We have the best life! Annie B. and I watch Mrs. Claus make grub for us from scratch once a week. It takes hours to put together, and if we sit close to Mrs. Claus, she always drops fresh veggies or pieces of chicken and says, "Oops, girls, I did it again."

That's our clue to each pick up a bite – what a great game! We do everything together: sleep in a huge waterbed; watch TV on the couch; go for walks; go to church... I never dreamed life could be so good.

The day my adoption papers came, Santa took the huge envelope and handed it to Mrs. Claus. He said, "I think this is what we've been waiting for."

As she opened it, she began to cry. I just held my breath, afraid that it was bad news for me. I don't think I'll ever hold my tail between my legs again after hearing the next words out of Mrs. Claus' mouth: "Kona's final adoption papers."

It wasn't until then that I realized that I had found my "forever" home and family. Now when I hear "there's no place like home," I understand the true meaning. I know I was adopted, but my folks tell me over and over again that I was born in their hearts, and I'm here to stay, FOREVER!

 (Kona, as translated by Jo Freeman, *aka Mrs. Claus)*

Just Fur Fun!

Never a Dull Moment: On her first day with us, Eva took one look at our neighbor's exuberant Golden, Riley, and bolted. Left holding a dog-less collar and leash in one hand, I was quickly reminded that there was still a dog on the end of the leash in my other hand - our yellow Lab, Flora. As she took off in hot pursuit, my feet flew out from under me off the wet Seattle pavement, and I landed headfirst on the concrete sidewalk. When I came to, my neighbor had Flora, but Eva was gone! Staggering home with a concussion and bruises, I kept calling out for Eva although my heart was sinking. But then, there she was, patiently sitting by our front door! Even in my daze, I couldn't help but appreciate how smart my new girl was – after only a day she knew her way home! At that moment, I knew, like the music of her jazzy namesake Eva Cassidy, our shiny Golden girl would never be dull! *-Glenda Guinn-Gilles*

Hansel, I mean, Parker: Parker loves bread, and can easily reach a loaf on counter. Thinking we were clever, we tried storing it in a corner swivel cabinet. It turns out that Parker is the clever one. Not only did he get the bread out and free it from its plastic bag, he left a trail of breadcrumbs through the kitchen and the den so he would be able to find his way back to the next loaf! *-Bill and Jane Littlejohn*

How Oprah Saved Gracie

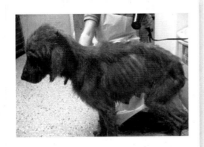 

It was Oprah's fault. All of it was her fault. If she hadn't done that show on the fate of puppy mill dogs and made me cry for hours, even days later, recalling the appalling visions of those poor dogs, I would be in the same rut with no story to tell.

My day started much like any other, though I got to leave work early. At home, on a whim, I switched on the TV just as Oprah's show about puppy mills began, and I was riveted. What I saw and felt literally brought me to my knees. Overwhelmed with sadness and anger at the plight of the dogs, my tears seemed to stem from a deep ache in my belly, and my eyes stung.

By the time my husband, Chuck, came home from work, I was red-eyed and runny-nosed. His dinner was extremely salty from my tears, and he was flabbergasted as to why I could be so upset. I told him about the show, described the horror, and argued that we should rescue one of these dogs.

We have a nice home and the means to support a dog, but he looked at me as if I'd said I wanted to vacation on Mars. I craftily took his silence as consent, and frantically started looking on websites for dogs in need of a good home.

At last, I spotted Gracie and fell madly in love with this pathetic-looking dog. The rescue website said she was a stray Golden Retriever, weighing a skeletal 29 pounds! She had lost a lot of her fur from mange, and had caked-closed eyes. As a therapist, I was most appalled at her atrophied muscles which prohibited her from standing upright, and wondered how she had ever survived. I was desperate to have her, love her, and keep her safe.

I showed her picture to Chuck. He was horrified: "Why do we need a dog? We just got rid of the last kid! We want to travel during our retirement. What do we want with a dog?"

I replied that I didn't need gallivanting or retirement; I needed my work and a dog. I called the rescue repeatedly, until they finally had to tell me (albeit nicely) that I was bugging them. They felt Gracie was in poor shape and might not even survive, but I knew in my heart she would.

Gracie got stronger and my emails persisted until one day, we were told she could finally come home with us. I was ecstatic; Chuck was not: "What if she dies? What if she emerges with a horrible personality? What if she eats my shoes?"

I had an answer for everything, and was determined to go through with this rescue. Although I was told Gracie's health was still precarious, I started buying everything she might need: A wicker crate; an orthopedic mattress (she was too bony for anything less); designer collars and matching leashes for all occasions; a life jacket so we could do pool therapy and for going out in the boat; every type of grooming brush and comb (even though I was not convinced that her fur would grow back); 88 tennis balls (a deal on Ebay); designer ceramic bowls; and at least 20 toys I carefully selected to be soft in her mouth. I was ready. She had to survive now.

The first Saturday in May, Chuck and I climbed into our Mini Cooper at 6:00a.m. and set off from Merritt Island for Miami (a three-hour drive) to collect Gracie. We were both quiet and entrenched in our own thoughts and worries. It was my turn to wonder, "what if..." What if she doesn't like us? What if she doesn't settle into her new crate? What if the blankets in the back of the car are not soft enough? What if I get pulled over for speeding?

Oh, oops - I had better slow down.

When we arrived, I was so excited, and felt like a new mom. I was impatient just to hold Gracie. I met Carol, the angel in disguise from the rescue group, who told me Gracie had opened her left eye for the first time that morning - she was not blind. I didn't care. I just wanted to meet her.

Finally, Gracie entered the room, and my life changed. She was so beautiful, even then, and had *both* eyes open! Her body was pathetically skinny with little fur, which made Chuck afraid to touch her at first because he thought he'd hurt her. Her sad face belied a friendly demeanor, and there was little wiggle in her tail. Chuck and I were hooked.

The drive home was easy. Both Chuck and Gracie fell asleep by the time we hit I-95, waking up about five miles from home. Gracie stretched leisurely and looked out of the window. When the car stopped in the driveway, she went straight for the front door and sat down to wait for us. When Chuck opened the front door she went right to her crate, sank into her orthopedic mattress, and fell fast asleep.

For the first few weeks, Gracie slept a lot. But slowly, she gained weight, confidence, and hair, and started to wake up. Now, Gracie grins. Our polite, friendly girl walks on and off a leash beautifully, usually carrying an important item, like a shoe, a toy, or a Priority Mail envelope. She enjoys lounging around the pool on the sun bed and has endured my attempts at water therapy (though she would rather just sunbathe). She loves boat rides (Chuck renamed his boat "Dog Hauler Too" and is Gracie's personal treats supplier).

Gracie is the perfect companion and just what I needed to get out of my rut. I can't wait to get home from work to see Gracie's frantically wagging tail and exuberant greeting. She lies on my feet when I'm at the computer and makes me go on long walks at least twice a day. She has even saved other dogs by convincing some of my friends to consider "used" dogs and not just puppies. In a way, Oprah actually saved Gracie, and then Gracie saved me.

 *Jo Ehrler*

The Royal Treatment

I'd rescued many Goldens from the County Animal Control, but it was impossible to keep a dog for more than a few hours because of my dominant German Shepherd, Royal. He'd have none of it.

Determined to do better, I erected a dog fostering area in my side yard, with a doggie door into my extra bedroom.

The day I finished the project, an animal control officer called, saying she had a Golden who had to get out of the shelter and that she'd bring him over on her way home. When she got to my house, she had to lift this little boy out of the crate. He was so scared that he peed all over himself and all over the driveway when she set him down. I led him to my new fostering area and left him to decompress.

Sometime later I looked up and there he was, slinking in the back door to be near us. Grabbing a bunch of dog treats to distract Royal, I corralled the Golden and put him back in the side yard, only to find that he'd chewed through the chain link fence!

The puppy escaped a few more times, and I was surprised to find that Royal wasn't the slightest bit bothered about him, so I told the Golden he might as well stay in the house with us. Several days later, when I knew I'd never have such an opportunity handed to me again, I called the rescue, asking to adopt him. They said yes, and I named him Foster, since that is all he was supposed to be. To this day, Royal loves him. Astonishingly, Foster has taught him to play and share.

 *Laurel Manning*

Voodoo Magic

I encountered a three-month-old, fluffy ball of fur named Tracy while on a trip to my parent's house. She was to be trained as a service dog by her owner, Mr. Marks, who was wheelchair-bound. Oddly, he didn't want me touching her, but I didn't think much of it and I never saw her again during that trip.

I asked about Tracy the next couple times I visited my parent's house, and was told that no one saw much of her. A lady who occasionally walked her said that she felt Tracy was being abused. I was horrified, and I wanted to find out for myself, so I called Mr. Marks and asked if I could take Tracy to the dog park. He said I could, however, I was not to give her any water or food. He told me he was punishing her with closet confinement, and no food or water, for four days!

When I walked over to get her, Mr. Marks said again, "Now remember, no food or water, and don't be too long."

Instead, I defiantly brought her to my parent's house, fed her, and gave her water. She was so hungry, and so thirsty, that I was afraid she would get sick from eating and drinking too fast. At the park Tracy cringed and turned her head away when I tried to reach out and pet her, and she hid from any man or dog that approached her. It was then, that I realized, the happy puppy I met a year ago was no longer inside Tracy.

Not knowing what else to do, I fed her again at my parent's house and gave her more water and a bath. She smelled awful, and her hair was coming out in my hands. I wanted to get her out of her situation, so when Mr. Marks came looking for Tracy I asked if I could keep her. I even offered to buy her, but he wouldn't hear of it. When I handed him the leash, she started crying and pulling away. He was literally dragging her feet on the pavement when her collar broke loose and she ran back into my arms, shaking. I started crying for her and for me because I felt so powerless to help her. Unfazed, Mr. Marks finally grabbed her and dragged her into his house. For her insubordination, he said she would spend a further two days in the closet.

Back inside my parent's house I called the local animal shelter. They said they would go out and check on Tracy, but I later found out they never did. To my dismay I also learned that Mr. Marks continued punishing her by keeping her in the closet with no food or water. I tried to explain to him that she didn't understand that kind of discipline, but he refused to listen, proclaiming he was an expert in dog training and obedience.

From my own home, which is a six hour drive from my parents, I called the shelter multiple times, the police, the Department of Health, and even the courts to get a court order, but they all were unable to help. The shelter told me pointblank that I watch too much "Animal Precinct" and they could not go to Mr. Marks' house. The police wanted photographic evidence before they would do anything, even though a neighbor had seen Tracy chained up in the garage by her neck with only her back legs touching the floor, while Mr. Marks punched her in the face.

Six months later, on another trip to my parent's house, I asked Mr. Marks if I could see Tracy. He agreed to let me take her for a walk, but I couldn't take her in my car. She was about 70 pounds now, not housebroken, and totally wild. I tried again to buy her from him, but he told me he would kill her before he gave her to anyone. He seemed to relish in talking about the beatings and food deprivation he used as "training." Apparently he kept her chained in the bathroom and put a full bowl of food where it was just out of reach.

I had to do something. I cried at night, thinking about what she might be going through at that time. How could I get her? Could I steal her? It consumed my every thought. I must have made at least thirty phone calls for help, to no avail.

One day I wandered into a curiosity shop while on a trip with some friends. We saw a voodoo doll and asked to try it, with all of us sticking pins in it. The owner of the shop said, "they work," and after the subsequent events that transpired, I, too, believe.

Shortly following my encounter with the voodoo doll at the curiosity shop, my mom called. She said that she was watching the police pull Tracy out of Mr. Marks' house on one of those long sticks with a noose around her neck. I asked her to get the officer's name and phone number so that I could follow up with him.

It took me two days to locate Tracy at the animal shelter, and when I finally found her, the staff told me they were about to put her down. I said, "Please don't, I will be up to adopt her. You know her story; I called you at least twenty times, begging you to get her out of that house."

After a huge ordeal, they finally agreed to let me adopt her, so my boyfriend and I took the six hour drive to pick her up. She was two-and-a-half at this time and didn't appear to have been bathed since I gave her a bath when she was one. Her hair was again coming out by the handful, and her ears were swollen and oozing pus.

On the phone, the officer who took her out of the house told me Mr. Marks had died five days earlier, and Tracy had been locked in the bathroom with no food or water. She'd eaten the baseboard for food and tried unsuccessfully to chew through the toilet seat to get water. She had somehow gnawed a small hole in the piping that supplied the toilet water, but the water was turned off and she was only getting drops. The bathroom and closet floors were both covered with hardened with feces, leading the officer to believe that Tracy lived in the bathroom but spent a great deal of time in the closet, too.

Since Tracy came to live with me two years ago, feeding time and bathroom visits have posed the biggest issues. At first I could only feed her out of my hand, far away from the food bowl. Now she finally will eat out of the bowl herself. As for the bathroom, she still won't let me in there alone. It's as though she wants to protect me from the torment she had previously suffered. She is four-and-a-half now, and is finally a normal happy loving Golden, aside from a couple of seizures. Her tail wags all the time, and she loves to play and swim.

Tracy and I have come a long way together. I never thought that a voodoo doll would be more helpful than the police, animal shelter, and Department of Health, but there you have it. Voodoo or coincidence, Tracy is finally safe in a loving home. Every time she looks at me I see the love in her eyes, and I know that every effort I made to rescue her was worth it.

 *Kathi Fegers*

Challenge is a Chariot

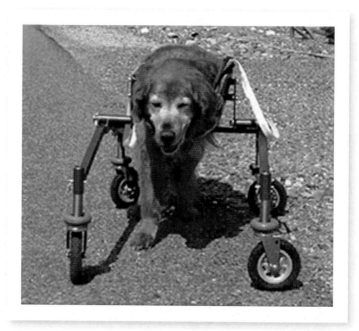

Hi Everyone!

My name is Trigger Boy and I am a 14-year-old Golden Coated Russian Circus Dog (just kidding) also known as a Golden Retriever.

My Mom says I should be the Poster Dog for why NOT to put your dog in the bed of a pickup truck. I had my front leg amputated after I leapt out of a pickup truck to chase a deer. (Oh, this happened BEFORE I adopted my parents here in Cody, Wyoming.)

Originally from Massachusetts, I was found on a playground and brought to a shelter. When no one claimed me, this young couple adopted me, and I lived with them for four years. We all moved to Wyoming, and on my first day here I saw this deer that had my name on it. I launched from the pickup, and that was a bad move.

Well, they said I had nerve damage and I would have to give my leg up. After the operation, I started growling at the three young kids I lived with, and it was time for me to find a new home.

My name was Tigger, but being in the Wild West now, my new mom changed my name to Trigger, and she says I am a pistol!

Since I couldn't keep up with my Golden brothers, the University of Wyoming Engineering Department took me on as a project to make a four-wheel drive "Waggin" cart. Four senior engineering students designed this award-winning device, and I got my wheels at a graduation symposium.

"Three paws up," for those brilliant students!

Two years later I crossed over the Rainbow Bridge. I don't need my "Waggin" cart here, where I romp with all the other Goldens, and wait for my forever family and friends to come play. See ya!

 (Triggerboy, as translated by mom, Carol Polacek)

A Yellow Ribbon for My Son

My oldest son, Jacob, joined the Army and went to Iraq with the Stryker Brigade. Six short months later, he was killed.

It was Jacob's desire that I should have a home. As a result, Jacob's generosity now allows me to live on ten beautiful acres on Camano Island in Washington State. The property is perfect for a dog, so I found Shadow, a Golden Retriever mix, to join me. He has since become my best buddy and protector, and has been a comfort through my grief and loss.

After adopting Shadow I decided that I wanted another Golden because of their gentle, giving nature, but also because Jacob had always said he would get a Golden when he returned from the war.

Shadow and I quickly discovered we had lots of room to spare in our hearts and in our home for a puppy. I found out that a local rescue group had just taken in a Golden with her nine puppies, so I filled out the paperwork and held my breath. I knew that raising a puppy was a huge endeavor, but Shadow and I were ready for the task.

We visited the volunteer's homes where all of the puppies were together, each with a different colored ribbon. They were all beautiful, and we were especially drawn to the one with the yellow ribbon around its neck. Along with many other applicants, we handled the puppies and learned how to trim their nails, hold them properly, and train and feed them, all the while sitting amidst these wonderful little creatures.

The day came when we were to find out which puppy was ours to keep. Each puppy was assessed to see which would be the best fit: temperament, response, trainability. I was thrilled to find out that I would get the puppy with the yellow ribbon – it was the one I thought my son would have wanted! I decided to call him Hunter, after Jacob's favorite author, Hunter S. Thompson. I know he would have approved.

Today, when I look at Hunter, I realize what a wonderful addition to our family he is. His playful antics bring a smile and some joy to those days when the loss of Jacob is just too much to bear. My youngest son now heads off to war, and I know that Shadow and Hunter's devotion and love will comfort me. They are truly a gift to the heart and spirit.

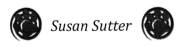 *Susan Sutter*

A Jessie of All Trades

Shortly after moving into a home with a large yard, I decided it was time to get a playmate for Jake, my nine-year-old Golden Retriever. I filled out an application with a local Golden rescue group, and about a month later got a call from Judy, one of their rescue coordinators. She told me to get to the Bellevue shelter fast, as there was a Golden there who was available for adoption. When I got there, it was too late; the Golden had been adopted. A week later, the call came again, and again I was too late.

When Judy called a third time and said, "Run to the veterinary clinic at Sea-Tac Mall," I knew that meant, "RUN to the clinic."

The dog I was about to meet was named Jessie, a two-year-old Golden Retriever. About nine months earlier, Jessie had been hit by a car and left by the roadside with her hip broken in several places. She was near death. The vet saved her life, spayed her, and had a veterinary assistant take her home for rehabilitation. Jessie was now recovered from her injuries and was ready for adoption, so the rescue group was called to place her.

As I drove from Bothell to Sea-Tac Mall in rush hour traffic, I promised myself, "I'm taking this dog, no matter what!"

So I did. Jessie was not housebroken, and she chewed everything in sight. She even chewed up the remote to the brand new TV, but Jake loved her, and so I forgave her various indiscretions. When I'd take her to the off-leash areas, I noticed that she was very curious. She would go through tunnels and loved to climb on everything. In obedience class, I mentioned this odd behavior to the instructor, who recommended agility. What the heck was agility? Who knows? But I called an agility trainer so that Jessie and I could find out.

I took Jessie over to the trainer's house for evaluation and found out that agility is a whole lot of fun! It consists of different obstacle courses with jumps, tunnels, A-frames, weave poles, and sometimes even a seesaw. In trials organized by the AKC, the "Standard" course is kind of the "smorgasbord," and the "Jumpers With Weaves" (JWW) course consists of only jumps, weaves, and sometimes a tunnel thrown in. The object is for the handler to coach the dog through the course as fast as possible, without faults. Jessie and I both thought it sounded great!

After a half-hour session of jumping over things and running through tubes, the trainer told me that Jessie was a natural. I got a second opinion from the Sno-King Agility Club to see which class would be most appropriate, and they recommended that she skip three levels and go directly into intermediate agility training.

In the beginning, Jessie was wild. I would unleash her, run to the first obstacle, and she would take off in the opposite direction and do laps around the barn - it was so embarrassing! After seven months of practice, however, Jessie was showing remarkable improvement. I decided to sign up for a trial, even though my instructor was horrified and certain I would waste my money.

Jessie ran the JWW course in 25 seconds, but knocked over the last bar. Later in the day she qualified and took third in the standard course. A month later she ran her second trial, double qualified, and placed first and third. She received her JWW novice title in just four trials and her standard novice title in only five, something that often takes much longer to accomplish.

One night in class, I noticed a classmate was wearing a flyball jacket. I told her that I loved watching the flyball dogs as they ran relay races over hurdles to get the tennis balls and bring them back, and she invited us to give it a try. Most dogs take one or two sessions of eight classes before they are ready for their first demonstration. Jessie was ready after only five practices. Her debut was at a Husky soccer game. Most of her practice had been done in an enclosed area, and here she was going to be in front of a large crowd outside on grass! To add to the distractions, the kids from the crowd passed up the seven other dogs on the team and ran up to Jessie yelling, "It's a Golden, it's a Golden!"

As the kids ran off, I thought Jessie might forget flyball and run to find the kids. I was wrong, and Jessie did great! Since then, we have performed at several Husky basketball games and a couple of Sonics games.

Recently, Jessie was picked for the flyball team going to New York to perform at the halftime show for the Nicks at Madison Square Garden. Philadelphia heard we were coming back East, and added a show for the 76ers during the same trip. We also went to Canada to perform at a Canucks hockey game.

During her flyball career Jessie has taken me all over the place. Once we went on a ten-day tour of New Jersey, Washington D.C., and Philadelphia! Jessie has changed my life and I am having the best time ever.

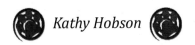 *Kathy Hobson*

Every Breath You Take

I have heard it said so many times when someone loses their companion animal: "I wish I had more time with them. Why are their lives so much shorter than ours?"

While I don't have the answer, I can tell you that it is not the length of time they are in our lives, but the lessons that they provide us.

One day, a one-year-old, tiny, blonde Golden Retriever was brought into the shelter as a stray. The shelter rule is a stray dog is held for 72 hours to give the owners a chance to locate their dog. This Golden came into the shelter on a Thursday, and a shelter walker (special volunteer that walks through the shelter regularly looking for Golden Retrievers) saw her and sent out her picture. The email said, *"He/she came in as a stray. Would not turn his/her head towards me. Appears to be depressed. Didn't have time to get more information, but I listed the Golden rescue organization's name on the dog."*

After years of doing rescue, I know Golden Retrievers are often depressed and timid in the shelter environment. Goldens are such social dogs that they seem to be impacted more by the stressful shelter environment then some other breeds of dogs.

By Saturday, the dog now referred to as "Eastside Kennel 28," had lots of drainage from her eyes and needed to get out on a "medical foster." A medical foster is when a shelter provides special permission to release a stray dog before their 72 hours are up. It is rarely granted, but we decided it was worth a try.

Early Sunday morning, day three: We open the door to the kennels and are overpowered by a blast of heat. It is June in Arizona, but the kennels are never this hot. Something is very wrong. (We found out later that the swamp coolers responsible for cooling this very old facility had died.) We get to Kennel 28 and there she lays, unresponsive and barely breathing. I pick her up in my arms and we run for the door, yelling, "We're taking Kennel 28 out on medical foster. We'll come back later to do the paperwork!" We break the rules, skip the paperwork and trust me, no one was going to stop us.

The ten-minute drive to the veterinarian office seems like an hour. We call ahead and the animal hospital staff is waiting for us and immediately starts to work on her. Oxygen, fluids, her temperature is 105.8 degrees. We now know she is a girl, and in the moment she's suddenly named Olivia. Yes, Olivia sounds perfect.

We keep telling her, "Livy, you have to fight to live. We will do our part if you will just keep fighting."

The situation is dire. Olivia cardiac arrests, but we bring her back. We keep petting her, talking to her, and telling her how special she is and that she is loved. We tell her about what her life is going to be like once she is adopted.

But no, there's another turn for the worse, and we have tell her about the Rainbow Bridge and how she will be at peace.

As she takes her last breath, I tell her I am adopting her. Olivia passes peacefully, no longer a stray, but my dog. Yes, my dog, if only for one breath…

In the animal clinic lobby quietly sobs an elderly lady. She has just had her 21-year-old cat put to sleep, and is calling a cab to take her home, alone. We take her. If not for Olivia, we would not have been at the animal clinic to help and comfort the lady. If not for Olivia, how many other shelter animals may have perished in the accidental heat?

As I write, it has been only one day since I lost my dog, Olivia. I let the sadness wash over me and I wonder the same question as everyone else, "Why are their lives so much shorter than ours? I wish I had more time."

So, rest in peace sweet angel, and I shall see you at the Rainbow Bridge.

 *Candace Ziemer*

Hardships Can Draw Us Closer

The past year was not our best. Charlie and I lost Moiré, my other Golden, to cancer, at the end of January. The day I took her to be put to sleep, she was still licking Charlie's face, and he was lying at her bedside.

Three weeks later, I was riding my horse, Ego Trip, in the indoor ring at the barn. He was simply trotting when he stumbled and fell. In a flash, I was thrown off his shoulder and my head hit a jump standard. Unconscious, I was rushed to a local hospital by ambulance.

I have no memory of the accident or the first ten days in the hospital; my whole life was completely unfamiliar. I didn't have a normal gait; I couldn't hold a coffee cup or talk the way I used to. I had double vision and my memory was clearly impaired.

One of the first things I remembered was my animals. I have two horses, two cats, and my wonderful Golden Retriever, Charlie. I adopted Charlie from a rescue group about a year and a half before this accident. My companion, David, told me that during the first week I was in the hospital I would yell, "Charlie, Charlie!" He would try to reassure me that Charlie was OK, but whatever he told me I could not remember from one day to the next. To reassure me, David had the idea of taking me to the parking lot to see Charlie, but the hospital wouldn't hear of it.

Ten days later, I was transferred to Heather Hill, a rehabilitation facility in Chardon, Ohio, which is staffed by incredibly kind people. They recommended that I establish a visitor's list of immediate family to protect my privacy. David finally got his way. The established list of visitors included, "Charles Lahner," my loving dog.

Charlie was a dog with a mission. He pranced all the way down the hall of the unit and finally into my room. Every night he greeted me with enthusiasm and love. He often whined, a sound I've never heard before or since. He always licked me and wagged his tail, and then after a few minutes of this great exchange, he would lie down right next to my bed and remain there until visiting hours were over. Charlie would not leave my bed unless I left the room. When people came to see me, he did not move. Charlie was friendly, but he had clearly had become my guard.

Coming home from the hospital and starting rehabilitation was frustrating and discouraging. Depression and fatigue are part of the recovery from a head injury. I felt like I had become a different person. Charlie didn't see me that way. He seemed undaunted by my tears when they came for no apparent reason. His only response to me was to be more watchful and more devoted. Charlie's presence at my side with his wagging tail made it hard for me to really feel sorry for myself and certainly hard for me to think about giving up.

A year later things are different. My balance is better so I don't grab the walls for support. I don't drop as many things on the floor, and my strength and speech have improved. As I slowly recover, Charlie is no longer quite so intent on guarding me. He still watches me and is always near, but at least I can be in another room by myself or go up the stairs alone. He must know that I am doing better.

The mutual love and devotion that Charlie and I now have makes me feel like I've had Charlie all of my life. But this bond of trust and love did not come instantly. Ours was a difficult beginning. He had been horribly abused, was untrusting, and we were both skeptical of one another. My accident was a turning point for us; it allowed him to trust someone again and reveal his love and devotion.

Moiré instinctively knew Charlie was special. She so emphatically chose him that I was compelled to bring him home. At the time I really wasn't sure about this dog, but now I think of Charlie as her gift to me. I can finally really see what Moiré saw in Charlie all along.

Peggy Lahner

Just Fur Fun!

"I'm Just Saying..." Jack greets us every time he sees us - even if it has only been 10 minutes - by grabbing our wrist in his mouth, whining, and wagging his tail. He also "talks," making more noises than I have ever heard any dog make. In the beginning, we thought he was growling and we scolded him. Now we realize this is just his way of communicating. These two behaviors together have become his standard greeting for the last three years.

Hot Dawg! When it is hot, Asher walks down the pool stairs, steps into the water, gets up on his back legs, and walks around the shallow end like a human. When he gets tired, instead of getting out, he just leans up against the side and "chills." All he needs is a pair of sunglasses and a cool drink, and he would be one cool dude!

Speak Only When Spoken To: Lucy is selectively noisy. She loves to roll across the family room on her back - growling all the way. She also greets us by barking when we come home, but only if we address her directly by name. If we just say, "Hi kids," she won't "say" anything.

"The DeVinney Dawgs" by Brad and Lori DeVinney

Little Brother Grows Up

My name is Bobbie, and I'm the only dog I know that has his own American Express card.

Some years ago, I found myself in a really scary doggie prison. Luckily, a few days after I arrived, a really nice lady let me out of my cell. She scratched my ears and petted me, put a purple collar on me, and told me I was always going to be safe.

The lady took me to a house where I met a dog that looked like me, but bigger. We played and played in a big hole of water in the yard where we got to get wet and catch balls! The big guy told me this was more like camp, and that I would not be staying long. I'd be adopted by another nice family.

He said he was my "big brother" with a very important job – he helps transient fosters like me learn the ropes. I thought he was just full of himself, but later I learned that big brothers *are* very important. He taught me how to behave so that a good human family would like me. He showed me what I could chew on, and what toys were mine. I thought the shoes were great toys, but he told me no. He also said no chewing on remotes, telephones, or wires. He showed me how to wait for the humans to come home, and not to run and jump on them, no counter surfing, and absolutely no accidents in the house. He said someday I might be smart enough to be a big brother myself.

I was just getting settled in and comfortable when this new nice lady came over to see me. I let her pet me, even though I was way too busy playing with big brother. Big brother said he heard the humans talking about me leaving with the new lady. This made me very sad, but the big guy said it was my chance to have my own humans, house, and toys.

It turned out big brother knew what he was talking about because the new lady returned a few weeks later, put me in her car, and gave me toys and treats. I was very nervous, but she seemed kind. We drove for a long time and finally got to my new house. WOW! I had even more toys there, my own bed, and I was the only dog!

I wasn't too sure I liked being alone with the human, but she knew how to play with me. After a few days, she said she had to go away for awhile. She left me with all my toys, food, and water, for what seemed like forever. But, after a while, she came back home and played with me again, just as she had promised.

One day she talked to me about bringing home another dog. Again, I was nervous because I had grown to be comfortable around her, and I didn't want to share her. She told me that I was such a super dog; I would be a great big brother. No way – really? I thought of my big guy and was so excited!

The shelter gave me my first dog; he was a real mess with no manners (I couldn't have been like that, right?). I showed him the ropes, and just when he was beginning to show some promise, some people came over and played with him. It was like déjà vu... I was sad to see him go, but quickly remembered that this is what a big brother does.

Just as promised, the dogs kept coming. Some were hard to train; others had no manners and ate my toys. We were helping so many wayward dogs that liked to un-stuff and de-squeak my toys that my mom gave me my own American Express card. The tradition has become that I always buy a new toy after our furry friends leave which means that I shop a lot!

A while ago we welcomed Holli, who looks kind of like me, into our home as a permanent addition. I've taught her how to be a big sister, and together we've had our paws full helping many dogs on their way to their forever homes. From time to time I think about the big guy and wonder what he would think of me now. I hope he'd be proud! He was right – being a big brother really is an important job!

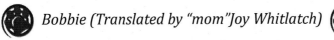

Bobbie (Translated by "mom" Joy Whitlatch)

"Tripp" of a Lifetime

Tripp tripped happily into my life from Tennessee Valley Golden Retriever Rescue (TVGRR), and a year later repaid us for his rescue with a rescue of his own.

My daughter, Sara, came to spend the night so we could celebrate my birthday the following day. At 3:00 a.m., Tripp woke me, quite agitated and anxious. I couldn't find anything wrong, so I went back to sleep.

At 6:00 a.m., Tripp woke me again, biting and barking frantically, and pulling on my arm. I awoke to the whole house rapidly filling with smoke, and I could barely see my hand before my face! Tripp ran across the hall and jumped up on Sara's door, barking and whining. As she ran from the house, I called 911 to report the fire. There were no flames yet, but I knew something bad was about to happen.

My vision obscured, Tripp pressed against me and guided me safely down the stairs and out of the house. The firefighters were already arriving as we exited. They entered the house immediately, and the second they walked into the back bedroom, the wall and floor burst into flames! My husband was at work on the news desk at NBC's affiliate WXIA in Atlanta at the time of the fire – imagine his surprise when he heard the 911 fire dispatch to his home address!

Afterwards we learned from the fire department that had it not been for Tripp's early alert, our home and our lives would have been lost in a terrible fire. Thanks to Tripp, the firefighters were in the bedroom when the fire broke through the wall where it had smoldered all night, and were able to put it out quickly. Tripp saved our home and he saved our lives.

The Cobb County Fire and Rescue Services honored Tripp and many of their brave firefighters at a banquet. Tripp was awarded "The Life Saving Award," and was the first civilian to ever receive it (not to mention the first dog!).

The news spread: Tripp received the G.R.A.C.E. Foundation's Hero Award at the Purina Golden Retriever Dog Show; he had the distinct pleasure of meeting Actress Betty White; he was featured as The Top Dog in Dog Fancy Magazine, and most recently, he was Mr. April in TVGRR's Goldens and Guys Calendar. Naturally, he was pictured with four of the firefighters that put out our fire!

Besides the fact that trip alerted us to the fire, there's one more thing that distinguishes him from other "normal" dogs. You see, Tripp only has three legs! As a stray, begging for food from local restaurants on a busy highway in Chattanooga, TN, he was hit by a car. The animal shelter that picked him up didn't treat his shattered leg, and three weeks later the decision was made to euthanize him. A Good Samaritan rescuing another dog overheard the conversation and asked to take him. They agreed contingent upon her getting him treatment. Her vet couldn't save his left back leg so he amputated it. TVGRR was called, and Tripp went to his foster home. No one wanted a damaged dog, and no one wanted a three-legged dog. But when I saw his face I KNEW this was the dog that would soon fill my heart with joy and our lives with much happiness!

There's no doubt in my mind Tripp is deserving of all this attention and media coverage – after all, he's a true "rescue" dog! We rescued him by giving him a home, and he rescued us by saving it from disaster!

 *Ellen Franklin*

Imperfect Is Perfect

This is a story about a dog that was not perfect, and a mom that finally gave up on being perfect.

I spent my days happily devoted to my kids, my husband, and keeping our house spotlessly clean. Even though the kids begged for a dog daily - or so it seemed - there was no room for dog hair here! Don't get me wrong, I love dogs and grew up with them, but I did not embrace all of the "dog mess" that comes with owning one. The straps of slobber, the crusty food bowl, the eye goobers, not to mention the ever present smelly bags of, well, you know.

What changed my mind?

Well, I hate to admit it, but watching the movie "Marley and Me" pushed me over the edge. This dog could do NOTHING right, and seemed to destroy EVERYTHING. But even so, he brought so much joy and unconditional love into his family's life! After watching this comedy of errors and accidents, I felt like I could put up with whatever a dog brought in to our home.

Grady came to us through a Golden Retriever rescue group. He had been bred to be a show dog, but was surrendered because he had a misaligned jaw and a canine removed - apparently he was no longer perfect.

Well, I beg to differ.

Grady has been the most perfect addition to our family. From day one, he has been sweet and obedient. We have taken him to dog training classes, and although he would rather "party" with the small dogs (Grady weighs 80 lbs), he comes when he is called, he heels when we say, "Heel," he stays when we say, "Stay," and he will even walk the agility ramp, just to please us. My seven-year-old, who weighs about the same as Grady, leads him around the class and Grady obediently follows.

I could go on, but suffice it to say, we love our Golden and all that comes with him. I have even gotten used to the golden rivers of hair that trail down the hallway from the front door to the kitchen. Imperfect is now perfect in our home.

 *Portia Gray*

In Sickness and in Health...

W e had just finished the training process to be a foster home for Golden Retriever Rescue of Wisconsin (GRRoW), and decided to ease into fostering by taking Dawson, a big sweet boy with no known behavioral or health problems. He'd live with us for a couple weeks before he was adopted, and everything would run smoothly. Dawson would be the perfect first foster dog.

When the foster coordinator dropped Dawson off at our house, he was laid back, walked nicely on the leash, and would lie down and wait patiently if I ever stopped to talk to someone on a walk. Our biggest concern was the extra few pounds that he needed to lose. We took Dawson to the vet a couple days later for shots and a check-up. The vet removed a few lumps from him, and a few days later we got the pathology results back. Melanoma. Dawson had four to eight weeks left to live.

We were devastated. He had only lived with our family for a week or so, but he had already made himself at home and we had fallen in love with our sweet big boy. I talked to the board of directors at GRRoW and they let me choose whether we wanted to treat the cancer or just make Dawson comfortable for his last few weeks. Treatment would be painful and would just delay the inevitable for a short while, so we decided to put Dawson in hospice care and have him live the rest of his life with our family.

Everyone at GRRoW was so kind, giving me the support and sympathy I needed. I had never had to put a dog to sleep but the vet said that eventually I would need to make that decision in this case. The cancer would not allow Dawson to die peacefully; it would slowly and painfully take over his lungs.

Weeks went by and Dawson showed no signs of being sick. After eight weeks we started celebrating every Thursday, the day he was diagnosed, for living longer than expected. In December, three months after he was diagnosed, my boyfriend proposed and we promised Dawson that if he was still alive he would be our ring bearer.

A couple of months later we decided that Dawson needed a birthday. We didn't know his actual date of birth, so we picked the date of his cancer diagnosis. Simultaneously we celebrated his 12th birthday and the six-month anniversary of his diagnosis. I sat in a chair in the backyard with a box of biscuits between my knees and alternated feeding Dawson and Elsa, our other Golden, as fast as I could. They are so devoted to each other that it's impossible to get a picture of one without the other. They're inseparable!

During his time with us, Dawson has become a completely different dog. Affectionate, he never demanded attention like most other Goldens. Now he's learned the concept of "fair" and believes that whenever Elsa is getting attention, it's only fair that he should get some too. Of course, we agree completely. If he wants attention, or if he just thinks you're not coming to give it to him fast enough, he will now get up and lean his 100+ pound frame against you for a full body hug.

After a good hug, Dawson's second favorite thing is bedtime. If he sees the toothbrushes come out he'll race around the corner to the bedroom, his huge frame crashing into everything so he can be the first to bed.

We had been getting the most out of our last "four to eight weeks" for seven months when I asked GRRoW about getting a second opinion on Dawson's diagnosis. At the specialty clinic, they agreed Dawson is a miracle. The first vet said she had never seen a dog live longer than four months after being diagnosed with melanoma, and the second vet agreed.

Dawson still had some suspicious lumps around his eyelids that we hadn't removed earlier because his prognosis was so poor, but since the cancer didn't seem to be spreading, the vet removed the eyelid masses along with a few others. The recovery was rough, with the hardest part was keeping Elsa and Dawson from wrestling after Dawson started feeling better. The pathology results came back and every mass was benign.

Although we did not expect to keep our promise, Dawson has upheld his end of the bargain, and so we will get married in a park by a lake where Dawson can take his place at our sides as our handsome ring bearer.

 *Kirsten Walth*

Just for a Week

During the catastrophic floods in Missouri, Love a Golden Retriever Rescue rescued "Foley," aptly named since he had been found in Foley, Missouri.

I laughingly now say, "Thank goodness he was not found in Knob Noster, Missouri," (a town close to rural Foley). What a doozy of a name that would be to saddle a dog with!

I really wanted to foster Foley, but our tiny house was already filled by our family and one dog, so when his foster family went on vacation for a week, I leapt at the chance to take him - we could certainly manage to make room for another temporarily.

I talked my husband Michael into saying "yes" to a second dog - just for a week - by informing him that Foley loved to play fetch. Michael loves throwing the ball for dogs, but unfortunately for him, our geriatric Golden, Annie, considers herself to be a human in dog's clothing. To her, "dogs" do silly things like chasing balls and bringing them back, covered in drool. She doesn't, so she must be something other than a dog...

The ploy of a short-term stay worked. My husband's eyes lit up. A chance to play ball! There were too many females in the house, and he and this male dog could do some "macho" bonding. It would be a nice change - just for a week.

Immediately, we discovered that Foley not only played ball, he was obsessed with it. He tracked the ball like a missile as he leaped, and dived, and skidded to precise stops. If we hesitated throwing it, he would frantically scan the sky after hurtling across the yard. If we picked up an orange, a wadded up shirt, or anything relatively round, he thought, "It's time to play ball," and then dance with excitement. In fact, Foley chose fetch over food - play time always came before breakfast.

When the week was up, we kept him in our care him, as I'd hoped we would, knowing that he would be snapped up soon. After all, he was a marvelous dog. It would not be long until he found the perfect family. And we honestly tried to find him a home. Really. He went to adoption events, he went on home visits, but there were no nibbles. Four months went by, and in those months, Foley solidified his place in our home.

We learned that Foley was very different from our senior dog Annie, beyond his unique obsession of the spherical kind. Annie would not think of getting up on the couch. Foley, on the other hand, took one look at the low futon and decided it was much more comfortable than the wooden floor. From that point, every moment that Foley was not playing ball or going on a walk, he was spread out on the couch. Smack in the middle, making it HIS couch.

Annie had never chewed up anything. Foley chewed everything. Thoroughly. Loaves of bread, leaving only minute bits of plastic as evidence. Disposable razors. Ink pens. The corners (just the corners) of throw pillows. You name it, it tasted good to him.

We had to Foley-proof our house, but it turned out we liked the "minimalist" look of our family room - no decorative pillows, nothing on tables that could be destroyed, as bare as we could manage. Doors were closed and locked during the day, keeping him out of the bathroom and bedrooms. All this, and we were still expecting that soon, any day, Foley would be leaving us.

Around Thanksgiving, my husband announced that since no one else wanted Foley, we "might as well" adopt him. Deep down, we both thought no one else would appreciate him as much as we did. When we signed the adoption papers, we became "foster failures" because we ended up unable to give up a dog we had fallen in love with.

It's now a year since we first brought Foley into our home "just for a week." He has made such a place in our hearts, we're happy to have him *just for a lifetime* instead!

 *Sioux Roslawski*

No White Flag Needed

"**N**o more, I'm done, time to move on to a new passage in my life."

These were my thoughts and words spoken after I put my Golden Retriever, Quincy, down on July 31st, 2008.

After 25 years and three Goldens, my husband Stu and I were ready to shed ourselves from the responsibilities of doggy ownership. Now we were free to fly across country to meet our newest grandchild whenever we wanted!

I was also turning 60 in October, and "too old" to start with another puppy. The training, the chewing, was a thing of the past. Hooray – no more clumps of blondish hair everywhere. No more endless paw prints on the carpets. No more water drippings all over my beautiful wooden kitchen floors. The house was clean... too clean!

The silence made me numb. The loneliness and emptiness was unbearable. I was in pain, unhappy, and detached. It felt like a part of my soul was chiseled from my body. I escaped by wandering the big box stores and malls; I went to the gym for hours to exercise. The memories rendered me incapable of walking the paths, woods and fields in my neighborhood. Just as the plaque stated, "A home without a dog is just a house," my domain was now a place to merely eat and sleep.

Someone suggested a small dog that I could travel on the plane with. Not for me. Once a Golden, always a Golden.

Finally friends intervened and hooked us up with Great Lakes Golden Retriever Rescue foster mom, Diane Missler.

Diane's joy of being a foster mom was contagious, and she found us the "perfect boy." Cubby was sweet, smart, mellow, and needed lots of loving. She faxed us his info, history, and a small black and white picture. He looked a little shabby and skinny, and truthfully, I was doubtful. But, it couldn't hurt to "check it out," so off we went. I was as nervous as a young girl going to her first prom.

We were delighted to finally meet Diane, and of course, Cubby. He was much more handsome than in his photo, and at almost two years, possessed a cute, quirky personality.

After our visit, Stu and I said goodbye and got into our SUV. But before the motor was started and the seatbelt clicked, I blurted out, "I'm in love. It feels right, can we adopt him?"

Stu felt the same. Less than six blocks from Diane's house, I called her, sharing our feelings with this incredibly giving woman - and it felt good – no, it felt GREAT! Cubby belonged in my life. I was to rescue Cubby, and Cubby was to rescue me.

At home I called all my best friends and family to inform them of our new addition. I still wasn't sure of his name. What kind of name is Cubby?

My son-in-law, Adam, was jubilant. Originally from Chicago and a huge Cub's fan, he knew this was meant to be. He sent doggy toys from the Cubs website, along with a Cubs collar which Cubby proudly wears today! I hung up the plaque, cleaned out the doggy bowls, and called the vet to set up an appointment. I filled out and faxed the numerous forms and adoption papers and called Diane a million times to check on my Cubby.

Cubby was Diane's 69th rescue, but she told me that it's always a rewarding and awesome feeling to release "one of hers" to a great family.

Since bringing Cubby home, my contentment has returned. Tennis balls in my bed, nylon bones and doggy toys throughout the house, and dog hair on my pillowcase. The soothing sound of the Dyson® vacuum brings balance to my world.

While the Cubs are chasing baseballs around the diamond, Cubby is chasing birds, rabbits, and squirrels in woods and open fields. The Cubs raise a white flag at Wrigley field to show when they have won. With Cubby, we don't need a flag;

his shiny two-toned, honey-colored coat reflects the first morning rays of the sun, reminding us every day that we are the real winners. Now every day is a glorious, golden day at our home.

(Dedicated to Diane Missler, one of the nicest humans I've ever met.)

 *Carolyn Tompkins*

Just Fur Fun!

Easter Egg Hunt: Dawson is a little slower than Elsa, so I let him watch me hide Easter eggs while my mom covered Elsa's eyes. Then they ran around the kitchen finding their plastic, pop-open eggs. Dawson's technique was to drop the egg until it popped open and then munch up the biscuit hidden inside. At one point, Dawson saw an egg and was going after it, but Elsa beat him to it. After that, he didn't want to drop his egg to get the biscuit out for fear that Elsa would steal it. He carried the egg around in his mouth for a few minutes until I took it out and opened it for him. Final count: Elsa 4, Dawson 3. But Dawson found the hardest one, which was in an oven mitt on the floor. This will definitely be a new tradition. - *Kirsten Walth*

True Blue: As I scrolled through photos of adoptable dogs on the internet, my wolfhound mix Rylee Moe decided to help. She looked at each one intently until I came to the picture of a Golden retriever named "Adi," at which time Rylee Moe suddenly started barking her head off. She barked so much that I called my sister to let her hear it! Rylee Moe's enthusiasm made my decision easy, and Adi (now Agatha Mae) became a part of our family. At first, "Aggie" was terrified, but Rylee Moe loved her like a true blue sister, helping her get over her fears and separation anxiety. Though Rylee Moe has now passed, her spirit lives on. Aggie continues the legacy of love as she nurtures the two neglected pups we've since rescued, just like they were her true blue brothers.–*Melanie Stelter*

Who's Your Daddy?

Ginger came to Golden Retriever Rescue of Atlanta (GRRA) from a lady in Birmingham, Alabama, who claimed to have "rescued" a stray female Golden Retriever that she was keeping chained in her backyard. Unable to provide the proper care or to afford the medical treatments that were obviously necessary, the lady contacted GRRA.

The lady didn't give us a name for the dog, so as part of the GRRA intake team, I began playing the name game with her. I don't know why I said the name Ginger; it just popped into my head, but it brought this ole gal to her feet and running towards me! Numerous other tests of the name were done, and each time she came running, enthusiastically wagging her tail to the sound of "G-i-n-g-e-r." Who knows how long it had been since she last heard it. Her identity had once again been restored.

Ginger had a number of medical issues, so my wife and I decided to foster her through her treatments. The most pressing was a mammary tumor about the size of a grapefruit hanging from her underbelly, which greatly affected her mobility. She also had heartworm, ingrown, irritating eyelashes, and cataracts in both eyes which rendered her somewhat sight-impaired. But all that did not seem to bother this loving Golden Retriever. She was full of life, affection, wet kisses, and greatly enjoyed all the attention being heaped upon her along with hearing her name spoken again.

Long before she finished her medical treatments, we fell so much in love with her that we decided to keep her as one of our pack. Her tumor was malignant, and we were told she probably did not have too many days or months left before she would be crossing the Rainbow Bridge. We were extremely fortunate nonetheless to have Ginger in our care for five months before she succumbed to her cancer.

She became a Velcro dog - stuck to me - and even in her last days, while unable to get around very well, she made the trek up to my second floor office. As always, she would come to me and look at me through her clouded eyes. I would say to her, "Who's your daddy?"

And with that she would do a play bow and lay at my feet. Of course, she would get a treat.

Towards the end, Ginger could no longer move around on her own. We carried her outside on her dog cushion each morning and gently spilled her onto the ground so she could hobble a bit and do her business. Then we carried her back inside where she would remain on her cushion the balance of the day.

One morning, as she got to her feet outside, she gave us the "look" we've seen so many times. "I'm ready... are you ready to let go?"

These decisions can never be made too soon, but they can be made too late. Having been through it before, my wife and I believe once the quality of life diminishes to hardship, it's time to say farewell to our dear friend and companion.

As we awaited the arrival of the vet, Ginger lay unmoving, quiet, and peaceful on her cushion in the family room. She seemed so relaxed, perhaps knowing that soon her pain and suffering would end. I sat with her, gently stroking her still-beautiful golden coat, silently thanking her for all she had provided us those past few months.

I whispered once more the words of our little game, "Who's your daddy?" With some difficulty she slowly lifted her head, turned it over her shoulder, opened her clouded eyes to look at me, sighed, and then placed her head down on the cushion giving me one final bow and goodbye.

 *Ray Toth*

A Beautiful Challenge

It was a cold day in January when we lost our beloved 14-year-old Golden Retriever, Maggie, to cancer. Heartbroken, we wanted another dog, but with two very active pre-teen boys, we didn't think we could manage a puppy as well. Instead, I contacted a local rescue group to find out if there were any older Golden Retrievers that would be a suitable fit for our family. The group connected us with a foster family in Wyoming, MI, who was caring for a very special Golden named Beamer.

I will never forget the first time I met Beamer. He had recently been rescued from an abusive home that left him incredibly mentally scarred. Even at 13 months old, an age when most dogs would be flopping around on the living room floor, Beamer was trying to hide behind the couch. He was a gorgeous dog, though painfully thin and incredibly afraid of people. He literally drooled with fear, and his body shook with terror at the sight of strangers, especially men.

That same day, we visited Poppy, another much older female dog that was also in foster care. She was everything Beamer was not - happy and outgoing - a typical Golden. We took to one another instantly, but I still could not get Beamer out of my mind. His eyes haunted me, and I couldn't forget the little lost soul I had met earlier. Before I knew it, we had adopted both Beamer and Poppy (who we subsequently renamed Bella)!

The first few months were difficult for all of us. Beamer was sweet and passive, but was struggling with a host of fear-based issues. He suffered separation anxiety whenever I left home, which manifested in the destruction of remote controls, baseball caps, and a Nintendo® Game Boy. He drooled when he became scared and ran from me when I called him inside. Things that set him off included men, brooms, fly-swatters, newspapers, and any loud noises. Crating didn't work because it terrified him, and the trainer we hired gave up, upon discovering that he would not respond to food. He even flunked the "shy dog" class I enrolled him in because he would not come out from under my chair.

I chose to ignore other's advice to give him doggie valium, and instead began to work on increasing his self-esteem. He loved other dogs, and so Bella became his protector and mentor, teaching him how to be a Golden Retriever. In time, he learned about car rides, walks, belly rubs, and doggie hugs. He quickly became attached to my boys, then nine and eleven. At their baseball and football games, he would still hide under my chair but learned to endure the attention of children who came up to pet him. Although he was uncomfortable, he never allowed his fear to escalate into aggression.

Beamer continued to respond to praise and love, and slowly began to trust us more. The chewing stopped almost instantly, and after six months, he even began to trust my husband. For the first couple of years, I didn't dare let him off leash as he had absolutely had no recall and would always take two steps back when I approached him. It wasn't until a family vacation three years after he came to live with us that I noticed he no longer left my side. When did this insecure dog become my shadow?

Beamer was, and always will be, my "heart" dog. One might say his birthday, September 11, 2001, was an omen for the rocky start he would have in life. Today, however, when I look at him, I marvel at the wonderful dog he has become. Beamer is still a very handsome Golden retriever who is just now starting to show his age. He has mellowed a bit, and genuinely enjoys his life with our family. Some might say Beamer was fortunate to have found us so long ago, but I know that we are the lucky ones.

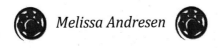 *Melissa Andresen*

"Lola, Who?"

One gray and drizzly Sunday afternoon in January, John and Judy stopped at the local pet shop. They had an excellent idea!

They thought, "It's been so long since we've "borrowed" Lola from (son) Niklas, let's get Lola's favorite dog food, so that next time they stop by we can ask if Lola would like to spend the night."

They would already have her favorite food on hand, so it would be an easy sell...

Judy paid the bill, and met John at the door. He said, "Oh, you must come see this puppy that just came in."

At the back of the shop was a lanky, clumsy, big-eyed, copper-colored puppy.

"Oh what a beautiful dog," said John, who immediately knelt to play with him.

The young couple at the other end of the leash, said, "Yes, he is quite adorable. He's just 11-months-old and his name is Micah."

After further conversation, they added that they were the foster parents, and he was a Golden Retriever rescue dog that had been surrendered by an elderly woman who was unable to care for him or exercise him properly. Here's the doozy – they also said that there was a young family and others who had already applied to adopt him. (Put sad face on John at this point.)

On the way home, John said, "Oh, what a wonderful dog. I think he would have been the perfect pet for us!"

Three days later Judy came home from work and found a voice message on the phone.

"Hello, John, this is Angie, Micah's foster mom. I'd like to tell you that the young family who planned to adopt Micah has decided to wait for another year or so until their small children are older. If you are still interested, I can put your name on the list for him and do a home visit."

Judy put the phone down and wondered, "HOW did Angie get our phone number?!"

Lengthy discussion ensued, encompassing topics such as: 1) Owning a dog is a 15-year commitment; 2) John is leaving in May for six weeks in Australia; 3) Lengthy international trips in the next eight months are planned; 4) The delight of having new leather furniture, expensive carpets, and a relatively clean, non-dog smelling house; 5) The master plan is to acquire a dog early NEXT Year! And so on...

Well, Micah came for a "home visit." John and Judy deemed it a success, and Micah gave them the lick of approval. So it was decided – Micah became John and Judy's unexpected dog.

"Lola, who?" Just kidding – John and Judy still love her visits, too. But now she has a playmate, and there's no need to stay over. Plus, Micah ate all her food...

 *Judy Christensen*

Aloha, In Every Sense of the Word

A couple of years ago a woman asked Golden Retriever Freedom Rescue of Colorado (GRFR) to take her dog, Dusty, or she was going to put him down. Since I lived closest to her, arrangements were made for someone to drop the dog off with me. When the doorbell rang, I opened the door and saw a young girl with a matted, smelly, overweight dog that was barely able to stand. She handed me the required surrender forms, but that was it. Dusty had none of the toys or treats that most other "owner surrenders" came with, and this woman even kept his collar and leash! She was lucky I mistook her for a transport person instead of his negligent owner because I can't promise that she would have made it off my property in once piece!

Dusty was in such poor health that my husband and I carried him into our house on a sheet. He was nine or ten years old, his eyes were swollen shut, and he had the worst ear infection I had ever seen. His skin was bright red and he was covered in open sores. Our vet discovered that at least three, if not all four, of Dusty's legs had been broken in the past, and had not healed correctly. Additionally, his shoulder had been dislocated and also never healed properly. He had an untreated thyroid condition and severe arthritis. Our vet confirmed that he was one of the worst cases of neglect he had seen in some time. When it was time to take Dusty home, we left the vet's office with more medication than my terminal grandmother was on before she died.

For weeks, as we tended to Dusty's wounds and medicated him, he would just lie there, letting us do whatever we had to. He ate lying down and slept most of the time. His only real motion was when he needed to go out, which he indicated by sitting up. To help him, we would slide him outside on a little make-shift sled/bed, and then assist him to stand so he could go to the bathroom with dignity. He never once had an accident; he never once got any on his fur. I still don't know how he did that.

Dusty seemed to be a shell of a dog until one day, we came home from work and he greeted us at the door with his tail wagging! He had walked across the house by himself, and I suspect he had been waiting there all day. His eyes were lit up... Dusty was back!

It didn't take long for me to realize that I wasn't about to let him go, and we adopted him. Every day his health improved through a healthy diet, vitamins, acupuncture, and regular massage therapy. Aside from the fact that he went blind due to Sudden Acquired Retinal Degeneration Syndrome (SARDS), I swear he is getting younger all the time.

After Dusty had become a bona-fide family member, we learned that we had to move back to Hawaii to care for a sick family member. The vet told me that, due to his age and blindness, putting Dusty in cargo on the plane was not recommended. Devastated at the thought of leaving him behind, I wrote to private jet companies, FedEx, UPS... searching for help. United Airlines came through, and not only put Dusty on the plane, but arranged for us all to ride in first class bulkhead!

At the airport, we were given the royal treatment. We had multiple escorts, porters carrying our bags, and they even cleared out the whole front of the airport tram for us! Just picture it - this cute "Oldie Goldie" lying in his special bed with his little toy, a blankie, and a flower lei, being rolled through the airport on a flatbed that read "DUSTY—HAWAII OR BUST."

Everyone stared, smiled, and said hi to Dusty – making us feel like celebrities. Dusty's little ears were perked forward the whole time, and I am sure he wondered, "How does everyone know my name?"

At the gate they let us *pre*-pre-board. Dusty walked into first class by himself and found a bed waiting for him, a crystal bowl with water, and a little plate with doggy treats and garnish set out by the flight attendants. The captain came out to greet him, and even welcomed a "celebrity guest" in his announcement. Many people wanted to meet him, but by then he had passed out and was snoring so loud that I had to wake him up to get him to stop. The flight went smoothly, we flew through quarantine where we picked up our other dogs, and within an hour of landing we were off to our new life in Hawaii.

The "Aloha Spirit" of Hawai'i is said to elevate and empower people. If that is the case, Golden Retriever Freedom Rescue has given the Aloha Spirit to Dusty. As I write, he is lying at my feet, sleeping, happy as can be. Though we are now miles away from GRFR's home base in Colorado, we will ensure that Dusty continues to be wrapped in the Aloha Spirit by filling his days with happiness and love.

Daniela Stolfi

Now She Laughs Out Loud

Our granddaughter Sammi, now eleven, was born with Alcohol Related Neurological Disorder (ARND)/ partial Fetal Alcohol Syndrome (pFAS). Children with ARND/pFAS are concrete thinkers, and often do not understand abstracts like humor, affection, love, compassion, happiness, or socializing. They also tend to have many learning disabilities, as was the case with her. Functioning in this world is very difficult for them on many levels.

Sammi lives with us, and never laughed out loud - not even a giggle - for the first ten years of her life. We didn't have a dog during that time, but I was raised all of my life with Golden Retrievers so I knew their capacity for love. I thought that the joy one could bring into our home might be just the thing that our family needed.

One day, my sister and I took Sammi to meet Charger, a three-legged rescue dog, in his foster home. The child sat quietly on the couch while Charger looked at us, jumped up between us, leaned on her, and lovingly and eagerly began slurping all over her face. It seemed impossible, but she began to laugh! Stunned, we adopted him on the spot. When we brought Charger home, he gave us a repeat performance of making Sammi laugh, and my husband couldn't believe his ears either.

Since then, not a day has passed without a burst of laughter or a giggle. I silently changed his name to Wind Charger because he truly is "the Wind who blows our sorrow away."

We soon adopted another Golden, Clover, to be Wind Charger's "sister." Her name became "Wild" Clover, because she always smells like sheets hung in the sun to dry. Just as Charger contributes to Sammi's happiness, so does Clover. She shows her that laughter can be about more than face slurps – it can be about games of chase, too. One of our granddaughter's favorite pastimes now is chasing Clover to get back whatever Clover has snatched (be it Sammi's underwear, my moccasins, potholders, or towels), but it's sometimes impossible because Sammi is laughing so hard. As our granddaughter giggles, Clover looks at her with bright, impish eyes, perks her ears, and invites her to begin the game of chase anew.

Charger, being a three-legger, has shown our granddaughter that "different" can give the world wonder and magic, just like her, and that she is capable of so much more than most people think. When Clover and Charger play, Sammi worries Charger will be hurt, but she sees how Charger bounds back up when Clover knocks him over. She sees them chase each other and knows that his three legs are just as quick as Clover's four.

We think of Charger and Clover as therapy dogs now, in addition to the family companions we love, which is another abstract concept they have taught Sammi - love and expressing love. We often find her hugging and smooching the two of them, an action she seldom took with humans; but she often comes to us now for hugs, too. Sammi's night terrors have disappeared, she has solid friendships, she empathizes, and her "frustration meltdowns" have all but ceased. The changes these two furry, funny, loving beings have helped bring about in our concrete-thinking granddaughter are endless.

My husband and I never thought that Charger and Clover would do more than superficially touch Sammi. How wrong we were. Clover and Charger have taken a broken little girl and started gluing her back together as she should have been from birth - one laugh, one act of love at a time.

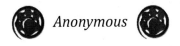 *Anonymous*

The Relationship Between Dog and Human

Our noble Max, a grand Golden Retriever, left us just one month before his 15th birthday. I didn't think I wanted another dog, but the part of me that said, "Well, if you already have one (which we did), you might as well have two," won out.

Living in a small town, all a person has to do is spread the word, and the thing you want finds you. When we put the word out we wanted a dog, offers of strays from all areas of the county came our way. The one we ended up adopting, a five-year-old named Lady Madalyn who was 30 lbs. overweight, charmed us immediately.

Since Blanton pets always have double names that are meaningful to us (except Max... don't know how he escaped it!) – Abby Rose, Woody Kitty, Cleome June, and Azalea Lou - Lady Madalyn became Maddie Sue. She was named after Peggy Sue, my favorite character, but in deference to her previous life, I simply added the "Sue" to her given name "Maddie."

It's hard to believe that Maddie has been with us for seven wonderful years. We've had so much fun together: agility training, games of keep away (where she would keep the ball away from me!), and long walks through the neighborhood. These days old age has made her more of a dog rug - a large mass of long golden hair - than an activity partner. Walking the streets to check out the neighbors is no longer possible; excavating large holes in the landscape is just a faint memory.

Chasing the ball and playing keep away no longer hold any fascination for her. Although she still likes to keep the ball very close, and, in homage to her younger days, takes it outside on her frequent forays into the backyard for bathroom breaks. Her old athleticism has been replaced by a penchant for listening to classical music with her human father. It seems, as it does for humans, music soothes her doggy soul.

Maddie Sue hardly stirs anymore; her eyes survey her kingdom from the best vantage point, the short hallway down the middle of the house. From there she keeps watch on the household activities and decides if she should move to get a better view. The shiny wooden floors are her enemy, and her feet frequently slide out from under her. But she continues her surveying, looking for a place to be closer to the action, sighing heavily and landing with a thump each time she relocates.

I know that sometime soon she'll be relocating to the far side of the Rainbow Bridge, but by uplifting her with love, I'll help her to land there softly, instead of with a thump. My best and truest friend, I would lay down my life for her, and I know with every thread of my being that she would do the same for me. Just as many say that the bond between parent and child is inexplicable, so is the relationship between human and pet. I cannot even begin to explain the science, but my relationship with Maddie Sue has demonstrated that this spiritual relationship between dog and human is real.

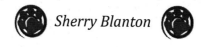 *Sherry Blanton*

Just Fur Fun!

A Successful "Foster Failure:" When two-year-old Ben came into our foster care, he was epileptic (with frequent seizures), obese, depressed, and unable to stand for any length of time because his joints were all stressed from his weight. He was an empty shell, with no life behind his beautiful brown eyes, and we wondered if he would ever come around. To our great relief, after ten months Ben's tail finally began to wag! He lost over 25 lbs., was able to get surgery to fix his joints, and his seizures completely subsided! Now playful Ben prances around with a ball in his mouth, just as a Golden Retriever should. He became our "foster failure," as we decided to keep him, but overall we would call him a great success! *-Chuck and Briget Wolf*

Parallel Parking: One of our rules is, "no dogs on the furniture," but Norman works it his way. Whenever someone sits down on the couch, he backs up to them and raises his rear end, one hip at a time, until he is in his or her lap! Once, when my mother was visiting, Norman "parallel parked" beside her. Imagine this dog, parking just his rear on the sofa, with his front feet on the floor... smiling at us! It was so funny - my mother and I laugh about that even to this day. *–Sally and Gary Meeks*

Must a "Real" Golden Retrieve?

When our Golden Retriever, Charlie, passed away, we decided that our three remaining mixed-breed dogs were enough. Several months passed, we had a lot less vacuuming to do, and the lint roller was sitting idle. However, every time we saw a Golden Retriever in a commercial or just walking down the street, our hearts were yearning, which eventually led me to my life's passion.

I was aware of Arizona Golden Retriever Connection because I had participated with them in the Fiesta Bowl parade. When the organization put out a plea for foster homes because they were receiving too many dogs, I answered the call. I did not know what fostering a dog was about but was willing to give it a try.

In walked our first foster, Harley, and our world was forever changed. Harley was nothing like our previous Golden Retrievers - Jake and Charlie were very calm dogs and real "retrievers." They retrieved toys, loved to swim, were well mannered, and would never even think of jumping up on people.

Not Harley. The whole "retriever" thing is still foreign to him. In fact, he doesn't even understand the concept of toys, let alone getting them and bringing them back to us. Harley avoids water at all costs, won't step outside unless we're beside him, and to him jumping up on people is an Olympic sport. We joke that if we have a party and no one leaves with a broken hip, the party is a success!

When we first took Harley in, we were troubled - this was not how Golden Retrievers act. We should know, we'd had two before. Then it hit us. We were trying to replace Jake and Charlie, but instead we needed to quit making comparisons and embrace Harley for the dog he is.

His shortcomings as a retriever became his "selling points." For example, because of his fear of water, we didn't deal with a wet stinky dog that developed ear infections all the time. Double Bonus!

We realized that he may not retrieve, but was instead silly, and his joyful exuberance surely made him a real Golden boy. For him, someone new - coming just to see him - was a reason to jump for joy. Turning his faults around worked so well that we immediately found him a home – ours! We had succumbed to what is known as "foster failure," which in this case was a very good thing.

Now we have our Golden "Retriever" and the story should end there, right? Well, I still decided to volunteer for this terrific organization that had found us the "perfect" dog. First, I just did transport, then I became Intake Coordinator, then Board Member, and for the last four years, President.

Harley helped me find my passion and has taught me so much about life. He reminded me that I can mourn the loss of something near and dear and hold it in my memories, but I can never replace it, and that is OK. He showed me that the "baggage" each of us carries can often be pried open to reveal a treasure buried within. He demonstrated that sometimes not conforming is a good thing. In the end, he has helped me to see that we are all guided to exactly where we are supposed to be, even if that means being a little different sometimes.

 *Candace Ziemer*

Nose to the Ground

Taken from his litter at five weeks, Dexter is a prime example of too early separation from mom and littermates. Unsocialized, he didn't like being touched, guarded his food and crate, and didn't bond to his owners and their children. After a few weeks, his owners couldn't cope, and surrendered him to Golden Retriever Rescue of Wisconsin (GRRoW).

I spent a little time with him and quickly noticed that he had a very good nose. He loved to sniff and had exceptional focus. I thought that in time he might be a candidate for search and rescue.

I already had three Goldens of my own and also fostered for GRRoW, so I really wasn't looking to add another dog, let alone a puppy. But there was "something" about Dexter that pushed me towards adopting him.

There were times when I wondered what I had gotten myself into. I dedicated most of my free time to filling his life with activities. A tired puppy is a good puppy! His lack of socialization made him fearful of a many things - mailboxes, noises, motorcycles - pretty much anything he hadn't seen before. He still didn't like being touched and groomed and was mouthy, rough, and pushy.

We did puppy manners classes, obedience classes, and lots of hands-on work at home. Mealtimes took forever, because he had to earn it by allowing me to touch him, brush him, or pick up his paw. I socialized him with people, cats, and dogs at my office. We took road trips to my brother's farm to crawl on machinery and smell awful stuff, to the gun club to hear gunfire, to the city for its smells and noises. We played endless hours of hide and seek games. I hid articles and he found them. He even found and retrieved a two-inch key chain out of three-foot-tall grass at five months old! When it was too cold or wet to work outside, I hid things in the house or at work. He found and fetched anything he could carry in his mouth - wrenches, flashlights, eyeglasses, and mugs. When I ran out of things to hide, I turned the lights out and let him fetch in the dark.

I was so pleased with his progress, I contacted a long time search-and-rescue person who looked at Dexter and felt he had a lot of potential. After receiving the "thumbs up," we decided to start tracking/mantrailing. For this, the dog smells an article with a person's scent on it and tracks the person until he finds them. The reward is a tennis ball tug and a party of happy people.

It took two years of hard work, but Dexter eventually earned his Advanced Mantrailing certification. Now we are proud members of the Wisconsin K9 SOS Search and Rescue Team. On top of his rescue duties, Dexter is currently training in agility, with an eye to competition, and recently started training in Human Remains Detection as well.

On the home front, Dex is a great dog, too. He would rather work than eat, and snagging tennis balls is his favorite occupation. He is also giving back to GRRoW by being a big brother to other GRRoW foster dogs.

Has he overcome the shortcomings created by early separation from his litter, and that lack of early socialization? I would have to say no. Dexter was lucky because he was born with some pretty special qualities that he could turn into a job, but we still work daily on the most basic skills to ensure he maintains his social skills.

The story does not end here. Dex will keep his nose on the trail and see where it leads, and I'll hang on for the ride of a lifetime.

Karen Stapleton

The "If's" Would Have Been Easy

Part 1: Rough Beginning, Hopeful Prognosis

Once upon a time there was a beautiful, young Golden Retriever named Zeus Bear. If this were a fairy tale, the ending would be, "Zeus Bear found his forever family, and they all lived happily ever after." Unfortunately, this is not a fairy tale: This is Zeus Bear's real life story.

One July Everglades Golden Retriever Rescue (EGRR) was contacted by Zeus Bear's owner. She was a mother with five small children under the age of eight. She told us that at two-and-a-half years old, Zeus was a yard dog and had never even been in the house. When the weather was bad, he would go under the porch. She also said that although Zeus was a sweet dog, he was destructive--he was digging up the yard. Further questioning revealed that he was not on any form of heartworm or flea and tick preventive, and of course, he was not neutered.

Zeus arrived at the vet's office freshly bathed. He was one of the most beautiful Goldens we had ever seen. He had shining, golden fur, a big block head, and the energy of an undisciplined puppy with a happily wagging tail. The family left, and Zeus was seen by the vet. Not surprisingly, he was heartworm positive.

We started the long and unpleasant treatment: Two shots, 24 hours apart, which kill the adult worms. The dog feels terrible for several days afterwards and must be kept quiet for about a month, while the dead and dying worms pass through the heart and lungs. Exercise at this point could kill the dog. After four weeks, an oral drug is given to kill the baby worms.

During this entire period of time, poor Zeus Bear was at the kennel at Clint Moore, because we did not have a foster home where he could be kept quiet. Finally, his treatment was complete, and he was neutered. Although he still tested positive for heartworm (that's how bad his infestation was), we were told that a monthly dose of Heartgard would keep the baby worms under control. Of course, a monthly dose of Heartgard could have prevented the disease in the first place.

We expected Zeus to be fine within six months.

Part 2: A Turn for the Worse

While waiting for his forever family to find him, Zeus had a seizure. In light of his history, instead of thinking idiopathic epilepsy, the vet decided to run some tests for tick borne diseases. Unbelievably, Zeus tested positive for Lyme disease, Rocky Mountain Spotted Fever, Ehrlichia, and Babesia. Any one of these diseases, if left untreated, could cause neurological damage and seizures, and poor Zeus had all four of them.

A monthly dose of any of the topicals like Frontline or Advantix, and/or the use of a tick prevention collar would have prevented these diseases. But Zeus Bear's family never protected their outdoor dog from heartworm, and they never protected him from ticks. Zeus was put on Phenobarbital to control his seizures and was given antibiotics in an attempt to cure most of the tick-borne diseases.

At this time, one of our wonderful foster moms, who had told us she needed a break, felt sorry for Zeus Bear and took him home. She quickly found out that Zeus did not have a normal reaction to the Phenobarb, and although he didn't have any more seizures, he became extremely hyperactive (this drug normally has a calming and/or sedative effect). He couldn't sleep, he couldn't sit still, and he chewed everything in sight.

There was no living with Zeus Bear when he was in this state, so she tried to wean him off the drug. Once off the drug, his wonderful, sweet nature returned, but naturally, the seizures returned too, in full force. Because he was unmanageable either on the drug or off the drug, he went back to the kennel. This time, the vet decided to specifically treat the Babesia, which does not react to antibiotics. This treatment was an injection of a drug that made Zeus feel even worse than the heartworm treatment had. He was pretreated with another drug to ease the side effects, and was given potassium bromide, another seizure-controlling drug. We all had our paws crossed for a happy ending.

Just before Thanksgiving, we received the terrible news. Potassium bromide was not controlling Zeus Bear's seizures. In a 24-hour period, he had several grand mal seizures, defecating and urinating all over himself. He bit himself and scratched up his face during one of the seizures, and our beautiful Golden boy was now a bloody mess.

The only thing that seemed to control his seizures was valium, which kept him sedated. No more wagging tail or puppy antics for him; just sleeping in his cage. We had an appointment for him to see the neurologist, but after spending over $3,000 on his medical care and boarding and on the advice of the vet, we decided to cancel his appointment. Since he had no quality of life left, we helped him on his journey to the Rainbow Bridge.

Prospective adopters sometimes question the clauses in our adoption contract, but they are all there for good reason: to be sure our rescued Goldens are properly cared for. If people are not committed to caring for an animal, they should not bring an animal into their lives. Neglect of any animal is a crime, and, in this case, neglect was the equivalent of murder. If Zeus Bear had been allowed to live in a house; if he had been given Heartgard; if he had been protected from ticks; if he had regular visits to a vet; all these ifs... but instead Zeus Bear, and those who came to know and love him, had to pay the price. It was not the euthanasia drug that killed Zeus Bear, it was the neglect he was subjected to in the hands of his family. They killed Zeus Bear, and we, his EGRR and Clint Moore families, are crying.

 *Hermine Scolnik*

Little Orphan Antics

After our Golden Retriever, Sonny passed away we were lost, but not for long. The Golden Retriever rescue group we contacted sent news about two siblings turned in by different owners. Having been an orphan himself, my husband Raymond said, "We can't break up the family so we'll take both."

There was Dudley, a gangly, nine-month-old teenager (or should I say juvenile delinquent?) who was full of energy. He loved to steal loaves of bread and jump in the shower with his foster mom. We named Dudley's littermate Dexter. He was shy, submissive, sneaky, and a little neurotic when we got him.

Dudley and Dexter got into trouble every time we turned our backs. They were so bad that a dog trainer recommended we keep them on leash in the house. We tried, but when my husband fell asleep on the couch, Dudley chewed through his leash and then through his brother's. Raymond woke up to find shoes and books eaten, and the house in a state of general chaos. Dexter was so sneaky! He knew Dudley couldn't resist chewing anything in reach, so he would bring Dudley objects to chew, and watch us yell at poor Dudley... until we figured out the truth!

The antics were endless. One day, I turned the water on for a nice bubble bath, only to find Dudley in the tub taking a bath himself! If that wasn't bad enough, one cold January night as I sat comfortably alone in my pajamas and house shoes while my husband played cards at a friend's house, Dudley kept taking an empty peanut butter jar out of the garbage can in the kitchen. To put an end to his game I took out the trash, and while I was outside Dudley managed to lock the deadbolt. Picture this: It's 20 degrees at 10:00pm and I'm standing outside in my night clothes, freezing. Luckily a kind neighbor drove me to my husband's friend's house to get a key. You can imagine my reception! Meanwhile, Dudley and Dexter didn't miss this opportunity - while I was gone, they lounged on our white couches and ate an entire box of dog cookies!

Little by little our boys grew up, so much so that we were eventually able to take in a foster. Our rescue group called about a dog that had surgery and needed some TLC. His name was Kmart because he had been picked up at a Kmart where he was running through the store with a pair of men's pants in his mouth. Someone finally caught him, and he was placed in our rescue group's care. While on the streets, he had lost a lot of weight and swallowed a piece of metal. Maybe he thought that if he got caught shoplifting, "jail time" would be better than life on the streets – he'd get three meals a day and a warm place to sleep!

We reluctantly agreed to take Kmart - what a pitiful little fellow. He weighed 43 pounds, was very ill, and had a bald tail from wagging it against the cage. We renamed him Dougie, and you know how this ends - he's been with us for years, has at least 20 toys, and is quite the swimmer. His tail is now perfect and he's a wonderfully sweet boy.

Our lives have been greatly enriched by our orphans, who have become our true family and given us far more than we ever gave them. Any sacrifice or lack of freedom because of them has been more than worth it. Any pain we suffer from their loss is a small price to pay for the unconditional love and devotion these wonderful dogs have shown us.

 *Gail Howard*

Nat-the-Cat

Life was never easy for Natalie. When she was six months old, her owner was arrested for dealing drugs, and Natalie was abandoned in his yard. Her savior was a woman who was a member of a Pit Bull rescue group in North Jersey. I spoke to her on the phone and she said that she didn't usually bother with Goldens in Animal Control because they are easy to re-home, but when she saw Natalie, she didn't think she'd survive another 24 hours. This rescue angel sprang Natalie from her cell and contacted the folks at Golden Retriever Rescue, Inc. in northern NJ.

The rescue group picked Natalie up and transported her immediately to a vet, where she remained for nearly two months. They determined Natalie had some sort of neuromuscular disorder, but couldn't pinpoint it. They also found traces of cocaine in her bloodstream! The kennel staff named her Daisy and as she got stronger, began taking turns bringing her home with them at night. Eventually, she was strong enough to be put up for adoption, despite her muscle tremors and difficulty walking.

We had applied to several Golden rescues and were thrilled when Bea Villa, Natalie's foster mom, called and said that she might have a dog for us. She told us Natalie's story and we decided immediately to take her, sight unseen. My husband, Peter, Brian (our son), and I drove for over an hour to Bea's home at the Jersey shore on a snowy Saturday. It was love at first sight when we saw Natalie. She reminded us of Bambi trying to walk on the ice - so thin and wobbly.

The rest, as they say, is history. Natalie grew stronger and eventually was able to walk fairly well - even run - and a happier pup you never saw. She continued to thrive when we moved to Florida and Natalie became a registered Therapy Dog, making weekly visits to a nursing home. Several other dogs entered our family over the years and Natalie became the undisputed matriarch of our little pack. Then, when she was about five years old, she lost the use of her hind legs suddenly and for no apparent reason. Again, none of the vets we consulted, including neurologists, were able to pinpoint the problem. But that didn't stop her – it didn't even slow her down. She learned to scoot around like a seal and we got her a cart for outdoor excursions. Nothing stood in her way. Her determination became legendary!

Sadly, one day Natalie's health took a sudden turn for the worse. She became listless, lethargic, and then refused to eat. The vet's x-rays showed that she had developed a condition called mega esophagus, in which the esophagus loses muscle tone, making swallowing nearly impossible. Ironically, it was this development that determined what her physical problems had most likely been all along – it was a neuromuscular disease called myasthenia gravis.

By this time, her quality of life had diminished and there was nothing that we, or anyone else, could do. Peter and I made one of the most difficult decisions that any pet owner faces. It was time to send our beloved Natalie over the Rainbow Bridge. She was a trooper until the end, and she touched the lives of everyone who knew her. We surrounded her with the people she loved most and helped her peacefully cross over the Bridge.

We will miss you, Nat-the-Cat.

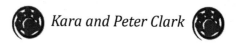 *Kara and Peter Clark*

Little Time, Big Love

A family wanted to surrender Ivy Jo, their 11-year-old Golden Retriever, to our rescue group. Why? She had diarrhea, was old, and they couldn't give her what she needed. They left her in the garage all day while they went to work so they wouldn't have to clean up after her accidents.

My Golden girl Meg, who was spunky as ever at 10 years old, followed me into the house where Jo lived. When we approached, Jo could barely lift her head and she whimpered as I petted her. Meg gave her kisses on her ears, and then left to inspect the rest of the house. When she returned and lay by Jo's side, I think Jo winked at her - that's when I knew she was mine!

The family told me, "She's registered. We got her from a breeder when she was eight weeks old. Do you want her papers?"

I kept my real opinions to myself, instead telling them I was sure this was a difficult decision. The 13-year-old granddaughter sobbed, as she had grown up with Jo her whole life. When I asked her if she had any questions for me she wondered if Jo would be in a cage. "No way," I told her, "She'll be loved just like my other three dogs. She can lounge in the house, on the couch, the bed, or wherever else she pleases."

Jo couldn't walk to the car, so the husband carried her and put her in. Jo and Meg had the whole back part of the SUV to get comfy. One the ride home, Meg lay right next to Jo as if to comfort her, and I really wondered if Jo would survive the night.

Less than an hour after bringing her home, we decided Jo needed to be part of our family and adopted her. Our three dogs accepted her right away, loving her like no other and making her feel at home.

It's amazing what a little love can do. That very next morning, JoJo ran, yes RAN, through the meadow with her brothers and sister! She dug under the yucca plants, so sure she would find a bunny. She trotted alongside Meg on our morning hike. She played with stuffed toys, fetched, cuddled, and loved us all.

Less than a month later, we laid JoJo to rest. It happened quickly - one day she was running and playing and two days later we knew it was her time. Those last couple of nights we all - me and my husband, her brothers, Pierce and Buddy, and her sister, Meg - slept on the dog beds by her side. I had kept in touch with the granddaughter who said it best - Jo got to spend her last days living "like a real dog."

JoJo has a special place in our hearts. Although she was only part of our family for a short time, she will be a part of our memories, and our lives, forever. Love you JoJo!

 *Shereen Raucci*

Dry Toast

When we first got him, Toast had:

- No hair on his cracking, bleeding, brittle tail and black hair on his snout
- Pancreatitis, very low thyroid, and a staph infection all over his skin
- Fear of everyone, never been part of a pack
- The smell of an old barn
- Never played ball, carried toys, or eaten ice cream

Oh, and water is only for drinking, right?

Wet Toast

These days, Toast has:

- A beautiful tail and full, fluffy coat, white hair on his snout
- No more meds, except for thyroid
- Belly rubs and pack playtime
- The smell of shampoo
- Big smiles
- Playtime with balls and toys, and ice cream treats

Oh, and water is for swimming, too - fun!

Patience makes good things pop... Like Toast!

 *Jan Mahoney*

Because Giving Them Up Is a Gift

Bob and I are retired schoolteachers and are currently on foster dogs number 78 and 79. Each and every one has touched our hearts.

The most common question we get asked is, "Isn't it hard to give them up?" Of course we fall in love with each and every dog. We miss them, and worry about them when they go out the door, but then we get our phone call with the first report. As soon as I hear the magic words, "We love our new dog," a smile comes into my heart, and I quit worrying. If only we could bottle that feeling... it's like a gift.

The following two journal entries highlight the reasons why we love to take dogs in and why we feel we must let them go.

Diane and Bob Missler

***

(Jeff adopted Luci from a family that had a child who abused her. When Jeff had a child of his own, he had to re-home Luci because she couldn't get over her fear of children. He writes...)

I make this entry with a heavy heart. It's been four-and-a-half years since she became part of our family, and tonight is the last night that Luci will to be with us. Tomorrow we journey to Michigan to surrender her to the Great Lakes Golden Retriever Rescue.

Diane and Bob will foster her until they can find her a suitable home. I hope it doesn't take too long, because Luci deserves to be somewhere where she can lead a relaxing life.

That place used to be here, but since the birth of my daughter, Luci has lived in her own little hell. It is clear that she is fearful of Hallie. I don't know what happened to her when she was at her first home, but it was not good.

When she is not fearful, she is the best dog. She listens, she's smart, she's sweet, and she loves affection. Outside of my wife and daughter, she and her "sister" Sadie are my best friends. I love having them with me when I run. I especially enjoy watching them run off leash. It is magical for me.

I feel as if I am taking a family member and giving her away tomorrow, and I'm going to miss many things about her. I'll miss the feel of her fur - she has the softest coat. I'll miss her unique sweet dog smell. I'll miss her coming to me in the middle of the night to have her head rubbed, and then going back to sleep under the bed. I'll miss having her lie on the floor in the basement as I do laundry. I'll miss her stealing clothes or shoes and carrying them all over the house - they usually end up under the bed. I'll miss her playfulness - she loves to run and play in the backyard, and especially likes to catch the Frisbee.

All that being said, she needs to go someplace where there are no children; a place where she can run, play, and not be fearful of her surroundings. She needs to remain active. I believe Diane is going to do everything in her power to put her in a Forever Home. Luci has led a challenging life, and I want her to go somewhere and live out her life in peace.

"LUCI, I WILL MISS YOU DEARLY!" Deep down, I know you will be better off away from here. Life here is just too stressful for you. I hope you end up in a place that makes you happier than you were here these last few years.

As I end this entry, she is walking around the house with a pair of my socks in her mouth. So typical.

***

(From Luci's new forever family.)

Dear Luci,

It's hard to imagine, but only a month-and-a-half ago, we were complete strangers. You were the smiling, furry face plastered on the pet finding website. You were a couple ominous paragraphs that spoke to Mom and made her announce, "I think this is the right dog. I think she needs us just like we need her."

We were the mismatched, nervous group that came to see you at Diane's house. We were the ones who fed you carrots and silently prayed that you would like us.

And then something magical happened – you became the newest member of our family.

Seemingly overnight, you've filled our lives with energy and love... and walks, lots of walks. Whether it's a romp in the backyard with your partially deflated pink ball, or cuddling on the couch, you attack each moment with a passion for life that is entirely infectious. You manage to remind us of the importance of finding joy in the little things like chewing on a well-loved Frisbee or touching noses with the neighbor's cat, and you do it all with that wide grin on your face.

Luci, we know it hasn't been an easy adaptation for you. Four homes in five years is something that no dog should go through. Your sad eyes and little quirks are evidence of just what kind of things you've been through. We might not always understand your oddities, but we understand your needs, and we are all committed to giving you the home that you deserve.

There isn't much left to say, Luci, except, "Thank you." Thank you for choosing us as your family. Thank you for loving us with your big, furry heart. Thank you for all the wet slobbery kisses and spontaneous high fives that make us smile. Thank you for this incredible adventure that we're all in together.

 *Love, Your new family*

A Golden's Favorite Treat

My three Goldens LOVE ice cream, but one of my "kids" is sensitive to many ingredients. It's always challenging to find something he likes that isn't full of artificial junk and chemicals.

Their favorite treat is a frozen yogurt snack I make for them – it's perfect for summer!

Ingredients:

- *Unsweetened organic applesauce*

- *Unsweetened sugar-free/unsalted organic peanut butter (absolutely NO artificial sweeteners – they are deadly!)*

- *Organic plain non-fat yogurt*

Mix equal parts of all three ingredients. Place spoonfuls in small two ounce cups and freeze. Once they are frozen, just pop them out of the cups and give to your dogs!

Note: If you have small breed dogs, you can make smaller portions. You can also use an ice cube tray to avoid added trash from disposable cups – a simple way for your dog to be healthy and "green" at the same time! *–Lisa Givan*

Woof!

Golden Learning Opportunities

The Ringer: Merlin, though not born so, was so good at being blind he fooled the shelter. Once passed into rescue care, his disability was discovered, but bells turned out to be Merlin's "guiding light." My other Goldens and I wore bells so he always knew where we were. He also chased balls with bells and could easily track where they were rolling. Between the bells and his instinct, Merlin was able to trick anyone. He quickly became the pack leader on our walks once he had the neighborhood mapped, and when I would ask people if they could pick which dog in the pack was blind, and they never picked Merlin! Merlin taught me that life gives us many gifts and we have to be able to see with more than our eyes.
-Christine Orantes

She's in Good Paws: Abby was adopted out, and then returned to rescue because she was afraid of everything. As a puppy she had not been socialized, and her breeder "loved her so much" that he offered to shoot her if the rescue group didn't pick her up immediately. As a result, common things like doors, coming in the house, and noises were terrifying for her. We were happy to find out that the key to her rehabilitation didn't lie in our hands; instead, it was within our girl's (our other Golden's) paws! They took over and helped Abby get settled in a way we never could have. Now, a year later she is so content that she sleeps with us and does the happy dance with the girls when we come home.
-Jean Gamble

Golden Learning Opportunities

Jolly Green Giant Style Weight-Loss: Max was 128 lbs., and had such a bad case of bilateral hip dysplasia that I had to drag him from room to room in his dog bed. In order for him to have surgery he had to lose 25 lbs., which I was told would take four to six months. Not in my house – we had the green bean diet! Replacing much of Max's diet with green beans helped him to stay full with fewer calories during his crash diet. Thanks to the green bean diet, and the dog lovers and rangers at Chatfield State Park who helped me carry soaking wet Max from the lake to the car every day so he could "swim himself trim," we made it happen in 30 days!
-Christy Cooper

Early Detection is Key: Every year the Evergreen Golden Retriever Club sponsors an eye clinic to screen for Pigmentary Uveitis, an eye disease that affects approximately 25% of all Goldens. We had Mandy screened when she was four years old, the youngest age we could, and while shocked to find out that she has it, we were relieved to have found it early. **Left untreated, some cases of Pigmentary Uveitis will progress to the point that the dog goes blind, and in a few cases, it will become so painful that the eyes actually have to be removed.** This is luckily not the case for Mandy - daily eye drops should save her sight, prevent complications, and allow her to continue to be the active, happy dog she is.
-Nancy C. Kiesler

To Save One

I rescued a human today.

Her eyes met mine as she walked down the corridor, peering apprehensively into the kennels. I felt her need instantly, and knew I had to help her.

I wagged my tail, not too exuberantly, so she wouldn't be afraid.

As she stopped by my kennel, I blocked her view from a little accident I had in the back of my cage. I didn't want her to know that I hadn't been walked today. Sometimes the shelter keepers get too busy, and I didn't want her to think poorly of them.

As she read my kennel card, I hoped she wouldn't feel sad about my past. I only have the future to look forward to, and I want to make a difference in someone's life.

She got down on her knees and made little kissy sounds at me, so I shoved my shoulder and side of my head up against the bars to comfort her. Gentle fingertips caressed my neck; she was desperate for companionship. A tear fell down her cheek, and I raised my paw to assure her that all would be well.

Soon my kennel door opened, and her smile was so bright that I instantly jumped into her arms.

I promised to keep her safe.

I promised to always be by her side.

I promised to do everything I could to keep that radiant smile and sparkle in her eyes.

So many humans to save. I was so fortunate that she came down my corridor; at least I could save one.

I rescued a human today.

 *Contributed by Golden Rescue South Florida*

About Happy Tails Books™

Happy Tails Books™ was created to help support animal rescue efforts by showcasing the love, happiness, and joy adopted dogs have to offer. With the help of animal rescue groups, stories are submitted by people who have adopted dogs, and then Happy Tails Books™ compiles them into breed-specific and region-specific books. These books serve not only to entertain, but also to educate readers about dog adoption and the characteristics of each specific type of dog. Happy Tails Books™ donates a significant portion of proceeds back to the rescue groups who help gather stories for the books.

 Happy Tails Books™

To submit a story or learn about other books Happy Tails Books™ publishes, please visit our website at http://happytailsbooks.com.

We're Writing Books about ALL of Your Favorite Dogs!

Schnauzer Chihuahua Golden Retriever PUG
DACHSHUND German Shepherd Collie Boxer
Labrador Retriever Huskey Beagle ALL AMERICAN
Border Collie Pit Bull Terrier Shih Tzu Miniature Pinscher
Chow Chow Australian Shepherd Rottweiler Greyhound
Boston Terrier Jack Russell Poodle Cocker Spaniel
Doberman Pinscher Yorkie SHEEPDOG
GREAT DANE ST. BERNARD Pointer Blue Heeler

Find Them at Happytailsbooks.com!

Make your dog famous!

Do you have a great story about your adopted dog? We are looking for stories, poems, and even your dog's favorite recipes to include on our website and in upcoming books! Please visit the website below for story guidelines and submission instructions! **http://happytailsbooks.com/ submit.htm**